OVERCOMING NEGATIVE THOUGHTS

Think Like God Thinks

Gregory L. Cruell

ISBN: 978-1-7167-6781-4 (sc)
ISBN: 978-1-7167-6780-7 (e)

Lulu Publishing Services rev. date: 08/11/2020

CONTENTS

ACKNOWLEDGMENTS

I am eternally grateful for my wife and best friend Deirdre. I will never be able to adequately describe what your encouragement and support mean to me in fulfilling the call of God that is on my life. You are my Proverbs 31:12 wife that has, *"brought me good, and not harm, all the days of your life"* and I love you for the gift that you are to me.

I would also like to thank my Isaiah 43:4 sister in Christ, Yolanda Goins whose labor of love in the final edit of this book helped to shape and mold the truth of the principles and precepts within that will *"make us free"* (John 8:32).

Finally, to you the reader. As you apply and share what you discover from chapter to chapter in this book, you and I have the potential to make a difference in the world. And **YOU** make a difference one life at a time.

INTRODUCTION

Many scientists have agreed that the mind is the seat of consciousness and awareness, the essence of our being that further governs our character and behavior. One study reports that the mind thinks between 60,000 and 80,000 thoughts a day. That's an average of 2500 – 3300 thoughts per hour! Other experts estimate 50,000 thoughts per day, which means about 2100 thoughts per hour. Most agree that over half of our thoughts are negative.[1] Negative thoughts can impact behavior and shape identity. You may be thinking, "I am a positive person, how can I have negative thoughts?" Positive people can have negative thoughts. They just don't express them outwardly. Consider this passage:

> *"When thou sittest to eat with a ruler, consider diligently that which is before thee, And thou hast put a knife to thy throat, If thou art a man of appetite. Have no desire to his dainties, seeing it is lying or deceitful food. Labor not to make wealth, From thine own understanding cease, Dost thou cause thine eyes*

---

[1] https://www.successconsciousness.com/blog/inner-peace/how-many-thoughts-does-your-mind-think-in-one-hour/. Accessed November 3, 2019.

to fly upon it? Then it is not. For wealth makes to itself wings, as an eagle it flieth to the heavens. Eat not the bread of an evil eye, and have no desire to his dainties, For as he hath thought in his soul, so is he, `Eat and drink,' saith he to thee, but his heart is not with thee."(Proverbs 23:1-7, YLT)

The ruler *thought in his soul* although he did not vocalize it. He was not what he appeared to be outwardly. Outwardly he was cordial and hospitable to his dinner guests, but inwardly he was *thinking* about his invited guests in his *heart* and counting the cost of everything his guests were eating.

His thoughts paint a picture of his true identity and suggest that he lacked integrity and character. It is clear that this leader was not able to overcome negative thinking. A reason is not given, but I submit that a lack of character did not allow the ruler to overcome.

Further, the soul (the seat of our mind, emotions, and will) is a portion of our character, which speaks of who we really are. People who possess good character often have traits like integrity, honesty, courage, loyalty, fortitude, and other important virtues that promote good behavior. These character traits define who we are as people and highly influence the choices that we make in life. And the choices that we make in life are governed by how we think, or by the mind.

What is the Mind?

In Matthew 22:37, the Bible instructs us to *"love the Lord, thy God, with all thy heart, and with all thy soul, and with all thy mind."* The word mind in this passage is the Greek word *dianoia*, which is more precisely translated as *willpower or volition*. [2] Romans 12:2 says, *"be not conformed to this world but be ye transformed by the renewing of your mind, that ye may prove what is that good, and acceptable, and perfect, will of God."* Here, the original Greek word for mind is translated as *nous*, defined as *"the seat of reflective consciousness, comprising the faculties of perception, understanding, feeling, judging and determining."*[3]

The Amplified Version of 1 Corinthians 2:16b declares, *"But we have the mind of Christ (the Messiah) and do hold the thoughts (feelings and purposes) of His heart."* The mind is also *"that part of a person that makes it possible for him or her to think, feel, and understand things. The mental ability of knowing, understanding and moral reflection; the seat or place of emotions."*[4]

According to the Amplified Version of Proverbs 20:27, *"the spirit (conscience) of man is the lamp of the* LORD, *searching and examining all the innermost parts of his being."* The Voice translation says, *"the lamp of the Eternal illuminates the human spirit, searching our most intimate thoughts."* A lamp is not light in itself; it is simply a vessel that carries light. A lamp is dark until it is lit or illumined from fire outside of itself.

God lights the lamp (man's body) and gives him breath, searching and knowing our most intimate thoughts. The lamp of the Lord illuminates the human spirit (conscience) as it searches, penetrates, and extends into every part of the human body. It is this light from God that gives us life and produces the mind of Christ. Considering the preceding passages and

---

[2] https://www.khouse.org/articles/1996/119/. Accessed November 3, 2019.

[3] Vine's Expository Dictionary of Old Testament and New Testament Words, Wordsearch Bible Software 12, 2012.

[4] https://www.definitions.net/definition/mind. Accessed November 3, 2019.

definitions, it is important to understand that the mind is not just a collection of conscious thoughts, perceptions, and feelings.

The mind is a process that begins with the spirit and nature of a man and ends with our being, which is expressed by daily behavior, conduct, and actions in life and ministry.

A Mind Detox: Renewing the Mind

The mind can also be likened to a warehouse of our imagination, recognition, perception, memory, judgment, consciousness and is responsible for the processing of feelings and emotions which results in our attitudes and actions. Thinking is the part of the mind that makes the effort to figure things out. It makes sense of life's events. Thinking creates ideas through which we define situations, relationships, and problems.[5]

The thoughts that pass through our minds are responsible for everything that happens in life. For example, feelings are created from thinking or evaluating whether the events of our lives are positive or negative. Our predominant thoughts influence our behavior and attitude and further control our actions and reactions. Another way to view this point is that thoughts are like a video that plays on the screen of our minds. To make changes in our lives, we must play a different video, a video that lines up with developing and becoming the *"express image"* (Hebrews 1:3a) of Christ by the way that we think. Satan knows that if he can just keep us confused and ignorant

---

[5] https://www.definitions.net/definition/mind. Accessed November 3, 2019.

concerning the *renewing* of our minds then we'll continue to depend on our own thinking and feelings, and thus be guaranteed to be *"conformed to this world"* and not *"transformed out of the* world*"* as we live in the world.

How Do You Overcome Negative Thinking?

For the clearest understanding of how to overcome negative thinking, several definitions are vital. Overcome: "to get the better of in a struggle or conflict; to conquer, defeat or prevail over; to successfully deal with or gain control of; or to gain the superiority against or over consistently"[6]

Negative: "having the quality of something harmful, damaging, and unfavorable" or "being pessimistic; that which hinders and neutralizes, not tending to see the bright side of things, without affirmative statement or demonstration of the positive"[7] Thought: "the process of using the mind to consider something"[8] or the product of that process, such as an idea or just the thing that you're thinking about. How do we consistently gain the superiority over harmful, pessimistic, and damaging thoughts?

I believe the Holy Spirit desires to communicate to us that having faith in God gives us the ability to overcome negative thoughts. This concept is likened unto David in Psalm 23:4 *"Yea, though I walk through the valley of the shadow of death, I*

[6] https://www.definitions.net/definition/thought. Accessed November 3, 2019.

[7] https://www.definitions.net/definition/thought. Accessed November 3, 2019.

[8] https://www.definitions.net/definition/thought. Accessed November 3, 2019.

will fear no evil: for thou art with me..." The life of a shepherd in Palestine was filled with threats and dangers, and as one who believed and served God, David certainly faced many threatening circumstances and people. Valleys were extremely dangerous as snakes, wild beasts, and criminals lurked in their darkness. Yet in the midst of all his perils, David found one thing to be unfailingly true, the Lord as his Shepherd had been by his side and because the Lord was by his side, he would not fear! As you read through, ponder and pay attention to the truths in this book, know that the Lord as your Shepherd is by your side to fulfill the promise that "*you will know the Truth, and the Truth will set you free*" (John 8:32). The truth is that we can overcome negative thinking!

Think Like God Thinks

We must develop the character of Christ to overcome negative thinking. In Hebrews 1:3a, the writer describes Jesus by saying "*Who being the brightness of His glory, and the express image of his person...*" The word brightness in its original carries the meaning of "radiance and brilliance." The word express is charakter which means the "very stamp, mark, and impression—the reproduction of God" in the original Greek.[9] The word image means substance. Jesus Christ is the very substance, the very being, person, and embodiment of God. Jesus Christ is the perfect imprint and very image of God's character. Let's return to our original passage.

---

[9] Mounce's Complete Expository Dictionary of Old and New Testament Words. Wordsearch Bible Software, Version 12, 2012. Accessed January 4, 2020.

From Proverbs chapter 23 and verse 7, *"As he thinketh in his heart, so is he"* or who he really is. As we think like God thinks, we become like Jesus. We become the very stamp, mark, impression, and the reproduction of God in our behavior, conduct, and deeds in the earth!

When we learn to think like God thinks, God's thoughts will change our lives. How do we think the thoughts of God? It is the practical application of the word of God on and in our lives, which is having the mind of Christ. The Contemporary English translation of Philippians 2:5 says, *"think the same way that Christ Jesus thought."* The New Living translation of Romans 12:2 says, *"Don't copy the behavior and customs of this world, but let God transform you into a new person by changing the way you think. Then you will learn to know God's will for you, which is good and pleasing and perfect."*

This book will provide engaging activities to assist you with developing the skills needed to renew your mind and overcome negative thoughts so that you can think like God thinks. At the end of every chapter you will find a section titled Principles and Precepts for Transforming Our Thinking.

The aim of this portion is to gather the main ideas in a summary format for reflection and practical application. After reading each chapter and rehearsing the principles and precepts at the end, the hope is that this process will create a bridge of application for your life and ministry that will assist you to overcome negative thinking. Note that all scripture is given in the King James version, unless otherwise noted.

The final portion of the book is the epilogue as written by my dear friend, Bishop Roderick Mitchell of the New Life Church, Cleveland, Mississippi.

Included in this epilogue concerning *"Overcoming Negative Thoughts, Think Like God Thinks,"* is a discussion of (Genesis 2:10-14). ***"And a river went out of Eden to water the garden;*** *and from thence it was parted and became into* ***four heads.*** The four heads serve as four thoughts for overcoming negative thinking. In addition, Genesis 1:4-5, *"And God saw the light, that it was good: and God divided the light from the darkness. And God called the light Day, and the darkness he called Night. And the evening and the morning were the first day.* From this perspective, the epilogue discusses the symbolism of dark and light within the concept of our thinking.

Through the practice of the principles and precepts contained in this book, my prayer is that the Lord will revive you and breathe life into you so that you have an awareness that you have been created to be in the *"image and likeness of God"* (Genesis 1:27). My prayer is for us to think like God thinks as He intended in the very beginning.

We shall overcome negative thinking because our sufficiency is in Him. It's All About Him, Jesus Christ, That's What It's All About!

Chapter 1

GOD IS ALWAYS THINKING ABOUT US

"When you alter your thinking, you alter your life."

-William James

God Is Always Thinking About Us

When we hear someone say, *"I've been thinking about you,"* we feel encouraged by the fact that we are not forgotten, someone remembers, and somebody cares. The phrase conveys concern, well-wishes, and often it stands as an expression for prayer. This is the love of God in action.

God's love is perfect, faithful, unconditional, forgiving, sacrificial, enduring, refreshing, redeeming, everlasting, inspiring, hope-filled, gracious, and so much more!

It's never based on us, our abilities, or our efforts to be good enough. It's found in Him and His character because *"God is love"* (1 John 4:8). God's love knows no boundaries and has no limits and there's no place that His love cannot reach us. There is no place or time in our lives where God's love does

1

not cover us, no matter how many mistakes or failures that we have experienced. The Living Bible translation of 1 Peter 4:8 says, *"Most important of all, continue to show deep love for each other, for love makes up for many of your faults."* David describes the way that God's great love towards us causes Him to think about us in the Living Bible translation of Psalm 139:13-18.

> *"You made all the delicate, inner parts of my body and knit them together in my mother's womb. Thank you for making me so wonderfully complex! It is amazing to think about. Your workmanship is marvelous — and how well I know it.*
>
> *You were there while I was being formed in utter seclusion! You saw me before I was born and scheduled each day of my life before I began to breathe. Every day was recorded in your book! How precious it is, Lord, to realize that you are thinking about me constantly! I can't even count how many times a day your thoughts turn toward me. And when I awaken in the morning, you are still thinking of me!"*

The formation and birth of a baby is perhaps the most amazing phenomenon on earth! God's creation of each of us explains how He thinks about us and why He is always with us. The New International Version of Genesis 1:27 says, *"God created man in his own image, in the image of God he created him; male and female he created them."* The creation of mankind did not just happen by chance or by some physical laws that were already in existence that at some point began to form human life. We were created by God and by God alone!

Whatever the basic substances are that make up human life, whatever primal raw forces and laws cause human life, they were all created and put into operation by God and not by some impersonal force or energy bringing basic cells and DNA together. God and God alone, by the power of His omnipotent Word, created and commanded human life to come into existence. Our identity is in His divinity and we are always on His mind because God is thinking about us constantly.

> *God scheduled your entire life before you were born!*

The way that God planned, imagined, invented and scheduled all the days of our lives before we began to breathe displays the intimacy and intricacy of His craftsmanship. It has been said that the world's population is currently estimated to be over 7 billion people. Yet there is no one exactly like anyone else. Our fingerprints and voice patterns are unique.

Our personalities and temperaments are uniquely our own. Our gifts and talents are our own. In other words, we are designer originals by God, the original designer of mankind! When God made us, He made us unique and distinct because He drafted a plan, His purpose, for all of us! Everywhere we go, in everything we do, God is constantly thinking about us!

"Let him have all your worries and cares, for He is always thinking about you and watching everything that concerns you" (1 Peter 5:7, TLB). The believers of Peter's day were suffering terrible persecution. The point of the scripture is that God will always look after and care for us, strengthen and secure

us, provide and protect us, give us assurance and confidence no matter what we endure because God is always thinking about us and *"He knows the thoughts and plans that He has for us"* (Jeremiah 29:11). In the larger context of Jeremiah 29, God's people were in exile in Babylon for seventy years, and it was important for them to adjust to their environment.

They needed to settle down, build houses, plant gardens, marry, start families, and increase their numbers. The Lord promised the people that His plans for them were not to harm them, but rather to bring them peace and prosperity. The thoughts that God had towards His people were imagined, invented, and purposed in His mind in spite of their captivity. God just needed them to change their thinking. In English, a thought may be defined as the "process of using the mind to consider something. It can also be the product of the process of an idea that has the potential to become that which we act upon or carry out." What we act upon or carry out is a result of an incredibly unique partnership of the brain and the mind.

The Partnership of the Brain and the Mind

According to Dr. William Salt II, the brain is the central processing unit of the body and plays a key role in translating the content of the mind (our thoughts, feelings, attitudes, beliefs, memories and imagination) into complex patterns of nerve cell firing and chemical release.[10] The human brain functions through a network of nerve cells that interact with each other to communicate and process information to

---

[10] https://www.sharecare.com/health/functions-of-the-brain/what-relationship-between-brain-mind. Accessed November 1, 2019.

determine what we see, hear, move, think, make decisions and generally function. The brain is the center of all bodily activity, but this activity is processed through the mind.[11] The mind further refers to a person's understanding of things and awareness that includes a person's thought process. In other words, the mind is how we think, feel and respond.[12]

The brain and the mind are partners by God's design where both play a vital role in the operation of the body that can be likened to a computer. Most experts agree that the computer is faster at doing logical things and computations.

However, the brain is better at interpreting the outside world and coming up with new ideas.[13] The computer only changes when new hardware or software is added, or something is saved to the hard drive. There is an off switch for a computer, whereas the brain is always on.[14] We are always thinking. Even when we are sleeping, we are dreaming, which means the partnership between the brain and the mind is active and working! According to an article at Knowing-Jesus.com, there are 39 visions and dreams in the Bible.[15] All of the visions and dreams were imparted into the mind (imagination) of man by God.

The brain receives input from our five senses (seeing, hearing, smelling, touching, and tasting) that lead to a subsequent response or action in the mind.

---

[11] IBID. Accessed November 1, 2019.

[12] https://en.wikipedia.org/wiki/Mind. Accessed November 1, 2019.

[13] https://faculty.washington.edu/chudler/bvc.html. Accessed January 5, 2020.

[14] https://www.scientificamerican.com/article/computers-vs-brains/. Accessed November 23, 2019

[15] https://bible.knowing-jesus.com/topics/Visions-And-Dreams-In-Scripture. Accessed November 3, 2019.

Due to the stimulus provided by our five senses, thoughts or the process of thinking then occurs in the mind.[16] For example, when I touch a stove, immediately my brain and mind partner so that I think that the stove is hot. When I *hear* the sound of the ambulance, my brain and mind partner and I think that there may be an accident up ahead on the road. If you're walking outside and suddenly see a baseball heading toward you, your brain signals neurons, which communicates with other neurons or nerve cells that send signals to muscles in your body that make you think to duck. No wonder David declared, *"Thank you for making me so wonderfully complex! It is amazing to think about. Your workmanship is marvelous — and how well I know it"* (Psalm 139: 14, TLB).

In order for our brains to think, we need the nerve cells and neurons that can detect information about the outside world and can transmit that information to other nerve cells.

It's the transmission of information, the cells throughout our bodies talking to each other, that's the fundamental physical basis for how thinking works.[17] One study reports that the mind thinks between 60,000 and 80,000 thoughts a day. That is an average of 2500 – 3300 thoughts per hour! Other experts estimate 50,000 thoughts per day, which means about 2100 thoughts per hour. Most agree that over half of our thoughts are negative.[18] If we think 2100 – 3,300 thoughts per hour and over half of our thoughts are negative (Just think about that!?!?), then how do we get rid of negative thoughts?

---

[16] https://www.dana.org/article/neuroanatomy-the-basics/. Accessed November 1, 2015.

[17] https://faculty.washington.edu/chudler/bvc.html. Accessed January 5, 2020.

[18] https://medium.com/the-mission/a-practical-hack-to-combat-negative-thoughts-in-2-minutes-or-less-cc3d1bddb3af. Accessed November 1, 2019.

Thinking Like God Thinks–Think His Word

Second Corinthians 10: 5 reads, *"Casting down imaginations, and every high thing that exalts itself against the knowledge of God and bringing into captivity every thought to the obedience of Christ."* The largest nation in the world is not India or China. The largest nation in the world is our imagination. Therefore, the Apostle Paul says that we are to cast down contrary or negative imaginations and make them prisoners to the Word of God. The Voice translation gives this statement, *"We are demolishing arguments and ideas, every high-and-mighty philosophy that pits itself against the knowledge of the one true God. We are taking prisoners of every thought, every emotion, and subduing them into obedience to the Anointed One."* The word thought, as Paul uses it in the latter passage, means a design or purpose. In other words, what is the purpose of this thought? What is the potential action or outcome connected to this thought?

> *The application of God's Word to life circumstances produces a manifestation and transformation of the mind.*

The prophet Isaiah states, *"You will guard him and keep him in perfect and constant peace whose mind [both its inclination and its character] is stayed on You, because he commits himself to You, leans on You, and hopes confidently in You"*(Isaiah 26:3, AMP). Therefore, God says whatever we imagine, when our minds are on God, He will give us perfect and constant peace! Peace is the assurance of deliverance through hardship, accident, disease, chaos and affliction.

During the COVID-19 pandemic of 2020, I noticed that those who kept their thoughts toward God had greater peace than those who did not. The peace given by God is a quiet, restful soul; a sense of purpose, contentment, fulfillment, and completion.[10] What this means for us is that the application of God's Word to life circumstances produces a manifestation and transformation of the mind. The plans, the purpose that God has for us is to be at peace and we can only be at peace by keeping our *"minds stayed on Him."*

God's peace is the assurance of present and future security, deliverance, and success! God's peace delivers a person through all the conflicts, strife, divisions, trials, and temptations of this life. The question that follows is, "How do I keep my mind, my thoughts on Him?" One solution is to have purposeful daily reflection or reflective thinking about Him! It's All About Him!

The Power of Reflective Thinking

Purposeful, daily reflection or reflective thinking is a powerful, practical method for shifting our thinking away from the negative to the positive. When we think of the term reflection, our first thought may be what one sees when looking into a mirror or body of water.

For the purposes of this book, reflection is defined as "the evidence of the character or quality of something." Spiritually, reflective thinking helps us learn to think like God thinks rooted in the quality of His character.

Naturally, reflective thinking helps us and gives us the practical application of what we are reflecting upon. First

Corinthians 15:46 in the English Standard Version reminds us that, *"it is not the spiritual that is first but the natural, and then the spiritual.* Created in the image and likeness of God, it is important that we know and understand that we are spiritual beings having a human encounter. Therefore, naturally and spiritually, when we think like God thinks, we become the solution to somebody's problem and the answer to somebody's prayer because of the character of God within us.

Reflective thinking includes reflecting on our relationship with others. When Jesus said we are to love our enemies in Matthew 5:43-48, He was creating a new standard for relationships. Jesus explained to His followers that they should adhere to the real meaning of God's law (God's thoughts) by loving their enemies as well as their neighbors. A Pharisee once asked Jesus, *"Who is my neighbor?"* (Luke 10:29).

Jesus then told the parable of the Good Samaritan. Here, Jesus taught that His followers must demonstrate love to all kinds of people regardless of their faith, nationality, or personality. This also included their enemies! If you love your enemies and "pray for those who persecute you," you then truly reveal that Jesus is Lord of your life, furthering the mindset and practice of thinking like God thinks! The term mindset was first used in the 1930s to mean "habits of mind formed by previous experience."[10] A mindset may also be defined as a habitual or characteristic mental attitude that determines how you will interpret and respond to situations.

> *Thinking like God thinks is an invitation for the transformation, development, and cultivation of our mindset.*

As believer's, reflective thinking helps us to develop a positive, God-centered mindset. We must be determined to reflect upon each day (quality and character). This helps us to grow and mature continually both naturally and spiritually. It has been said that the largest room in the world is the room for improvement.

When we reflect upon a thought that is negative, the reflective thinking helps us to change direction from the negative to that which is positive. When a negative thought occurs, reflect and *T.H.I.N.K.*

- o **T-**is it true? If not, reflect and reject. Hit the delete button in your mind.
- o **H-**is it helpful? If not, reflect and reject. Hit the delete button in your mind.
- o **I-** is it inspirational? If, not reflect and reject. Hit the delete button in your mind.
- o **N-**is it necessary? If not, reflect and reject. Hit the delete button in your mind.
- o **K-**is it kind? If not, reflect and reject. Hit the delete button in your mind.

As you delete the negative thought, shift your mind to think of something positive. Thoughts like Psalm 139:14, *"I am fearfully and wonderfully made..."* Thoughts like Proverbs 3:5-6, *"Trust in the Lord with all your heart, and do not lean on your own understanding. In all your ways acknowledge him, and he will make your paths straight."* Thoughts like Mark 11:23, *"Truly I say to you, whoever says to this mountain, be taken up and thrown into the sea and does not doubt in his heart but believes that what he says will come to pass, it will be done."* Thoughts like Isaiah 54:17, *"No weapon that is formed against you shall succeed..."*

This is reflective thinking, which focuses on the quality and character of a matter, specifically on the character of God's word.

What matters in life and ministry is that our conduct and deeds represent the thoughts of God. We must train ourselves to think like God thinks. This is a part of the continual process of overcoming negative thoughts. To think like God thinks is an invitation to transform or simply to develop and cultivate a continual and perpetual mindset of "thinking for a change."

> *To think for a change is to think like God thinks because God can change things!*

Thinking for a change includes thoughts and mindsets like the following:

o *"Not everything that is faced can be changed, but nothing can be changed until it is faced."*

James Baldwin

11

o *"Everyone thinks of changing the world, but no one thinks of changing himself."*

Leo Tolstoy

o *"Progress is impossible without change, and those who cannot change their minds cannot change anything."*

George Bernard Shaw

o *"When the winds of change blow, some people build walls and others build windmills."*

Chinese Proverb

To think for a change is to think like God thinks because God can change things. God is always thinking about us and as we learn to think like God thinks, we can change our world and the lives of those that we live with, work with, and worship with.

"When you alter your thinking, you alter your life."

-William James

Principles and Precepts For Transforming Our Thinking

"And do not be conformed to this world [any longer with its superficial values and customs], but be transformed and progressively changed [as you mature spiritually] by the renewing of your mind [focusing on godly values and ethical attitudes], so that you may prove [for yourselves] what the will of God is, that which is good and acceptable and perfect [in His plan and purpose for you]" (Romans 12:2, AMP).

Principle–a universal law that is true in any context, situation, or environment.

Precept–life lessons indicating the way one should act or behave.

Practice–the act of rehearsing a behavior over and over, for the purpose of improving or mastering it.

Chapter 1 Reflection Practices

1. What principles and precepts have you discovered in this chapter that you can apply to your life in order to think like God thinks?

    o   God has made each of us uniquely.
        Can you think of a reason why it is important to be yourself instead of emulating others?

    o   What mistakes have you made that can be converted into lessons for yourself or others?

2. Knowing that God is always thinking about you, how does this impact the way that you think about yourself?

3. If you have had or are having negative thoughts about yourself, or others, what daily action steps can you take to change those thoughts from the negative to positive based on the content of this chapter?

4. What examples of truth have you discovered that empower you to think like God thinks?

   "Progress is impossible without change, and those who cannot change their minds cannot change anything."

   – George Bernard Shaw

Chapter 2

THINKING LIKE GOD
THINKS MAINTAINS THE
RIGHT PERSPECTIVE

*"The things you think about determine the quality
of your mind. Your soul takes on the color of your
thoughts."*

-Marcus Aurelius

Maintaining the Right Perspective

The term perspective has a Latin root meaning "to look
through" or "perceive," which relates to looking or how we
see a matter.[19] If we were to observe the world from an eagle's
perspective, we would see from the heights of the eagle's
elevated flight pattern.

---

[19] https://dictionary.cambridge.org/us/dictionary/english/perspective.
Accessed January 6, 2020.

Wildlife biologists and scientists tell us that eagles can obtain heights or altitudes of up to 10,000 feet. An eagle's eyesight is estimated to be 5 to 6 times sharper than that of a human. They are capable of seeing over 1½ miles away.[20]

> *We must train ourselves to think like God thinks to maintain the right perspective to overcome negative thoughts.*

If we say someone "has a good perspective," this can mean that person has the right outlook or mindset of life which includes the good, the bad, and the ugly. If we had a choice, everything would always be good, but sometimes we experience things that are bad. Life will have its ups and downs.

Life is full of the good, the bad, and the ugly and we must train ourselves to think like God thinks to maintain the right perspective to overcome negative thoughts. For example, it is helpful to think that bad experiences can give us a reason to appreciate the good experiences even more. When we think like God thinks, we focus on the fact that we are never alone through the good, the bad, and the ugly times in life.

In the New Living translation, David declares, *"I can never escape from your Spirit! I can never get away from your presence! If I go up to heaven, you are there; if I go down to the grave, you are there. If I ride the wings of the morning, if I dwell by the farthest*

---

[20] https://en.wikipedia.org/wiki/Eagle_eye. Accessed January 6, 2020.

oceans, even there your hand will guide me, and your strength will support me" (Psalms 139: 7-10).

God never said that everything would be good, but He said that He would cause everything to work together for the good (Romans 8: 28)! The bad and ugly experiences in life may not feel good or be pleasant, but there is a purpose behind them.

David also said, "*It is good for me that I have been afflicted, that I might learn Your statutes*" (Psalms 119: 71). Naturally speaking, I would say that's bad, but David said what I have been through is good! David chose to view (his perspective) his affliction through spiritual eyes, which led him to a greater understanding of the value of suffering in a believer's life. David declared gratefully that his affliction had been good for him, because it had stirred him to learn the power of God's Word in greater ways than ever before. The same is true of any trouble, trauma, or drama that we may have to endure. In most cases, we are not able to see what God is producing in us through the afflictions.

When we persevere in our struggles and look for God's hand in them, we will eventually understand that the Lord is compassionate and merciful and it's all "*working together for our good*" (Romans 8:28). This is thinking like God thinks!

Principles and Precepts For Maintaining The Right Perspective

The key to successfully and consistently thinking like God thinks is maintaining the right perspective or how we see a matter. At this point of the chapter, I would like to suggest several principles or precepts to assist you in maintaining the right perspective. The following portion of the chapter is not an exhaustive treatment of how to maintain the right perspective. It is simply a place to continue training our mind to practice precepts to overcome negative thinking.

Begin Each Day with the Things That Matter Most

Begin each day with prayer. We must never forget that prayer is our lifeline in our relationship with the Lord. My wife and I pray one of David's prayers to exercise this principle: "*Show me your ways, O LORD, teach me your paths; guide me in your truth and teach me, for you are God my Savior, and my hope is in you all day long*"(Psalms 25:4-5, NIV).

Begin each day remembering God's blessings. "*Give thanks to the Lord for He is good, His love endures forever*" (Psalms 118:29). God's love is the most profound blessing that we can ever experience. When we think like God thinks, we can pray, "*Lord, I have been having a hard time over the past few days, but I know that You are watching over me. Thank You for Your unconditional, unfailing love, and help me to never forget how you have blessed me and are blessing me right now. Amen!*"

Begin each day remembering family. There is no greater treasure in the earth than family. There is no amount of money, no amount of prestige or power that's more valuable than family. According to the Amplified Version of Genesis 1: 27 – 28, family is important to God. "*God created man in His own image, in the image and likeness of God He created him; male and female He created them. And God blessed them and said to them, Be fruitful, multiply, and fill the earth, and subdue it [using all its vast resources in the service of God and man] ..."*

However, every family is going to be tempted by natural challenges and issues. The first family, Adam and Eve, were deceived by the serpent (Satan) when they failed to follow and obey God. Consequently, they were banished from the Garden of Eden (Genesis 3:13-24). The nature of these issues is so prevalent in the DNA of humanity that conflict arose in Adam and Eve's son, Cain, and he kills his brother Abel (Genesis 4:8).

Conflict can cause the arousal of powerful negative emotions such as anger, frustration, suspicion, and insecurity. Conflict and disagreement are inevitable in families because the potential resides in all of us. But when we think like God thinks, we realize that conflict and disagreement can be overcome by love. In Proverbs 10:12, God reminds us that *"Hatred stirs up conflict, but love covers over all wrongs."* In what way does love cover sin? As believers we personify the love of God by forgiving others and thereby, we cover their sin.

Jesus admonished His disciples to love: *"A new command I give you: Love one another. As I have loved you, so you must love one another. By this all men will know that you are my disciples, if you love one another"* (John 13: 34–35). When we love each other, we are willing to forgive each other because love *"keeps no record of wrongs"* (1 Corinthians 13:5). When we walk in love and forgiveness, we think like God thinks so we become more like Him.

Begin each day remembering that you have back-up. Isaiah 52:12b in the Message Bible proclaims, *"For the Lord will go ahead of you; yes, the God of Israel will protect you from behind."* David said in Psalms 23:6, *"Goodness and mercy shall follow me*

19

all the days of my life." That is back-up! God will always back us up if we don't back down!

Begin each day remembering you have divine lineage. *"God has said in His Word and He will not change his mind; You are a priest forever, in the order of Melchizedek"* (Psalms 110:4). Melchizedek means "king of righteousness."

Our salvation is in the power of our eternal High Priest, the King of Righteousness after the order of Melchizedek, Christ Jesus our Lord. In representation of Him, our priesthood reminds us that we are *"a chosen people, a royal priesthood, a holy nation, a people belonging to God, that you may declare the praises of him who called you out of darkness into his wonderful light"* (1 Peter 2:9, NIV).

Remind Yourself of Your Priorities

There are also several ways to apply principles and precepts that assist us in establishing priorities.

Organize and plan ahead. Create a list of everything you have to do. Then, arrange the list in order of most importance. Even though you can't do everything at once, prioritizing helps us to figure out which tasks are the most important for our place of work or church. *"In his heart a man plans his course, but the LORD determines his steps"* (Proverbs 16:9, NIV).

Organizing, prioritizing and planning charts a course for our daily assignments and tasks but when we allow God to determine our steps, He also establishes trustworthy relationships with others that helps to provide the council on how to get it all done. *"Plans fail for lack of counsel, but with many advisers they succeed"* (Proverbs 15:22, NIV).

Focusing on each task, with trusted council provided by God helps to avoid frustration with our many and varied daily tasks and assignments. By improving our performance through good planning and preparation, we create a clearer direction about what to do next organizationally. This perspective reduces stress, increases productivity, and creates an environment that people are glad to work in.

Don't overcommit yourself. *"For everything there is a season, and a time for every matter under heaven"* (Ecclesiastes 3:1). The habit of saying "yes" to every project that comes your way is a tough one to break.

If you want to take on a new project, stop to think through how you'd need to re-prioritize your current responsibilities to complete it. Determine the steps you'd need to take and the time you'd be able to spend on it. Be realistic in your estimates and don't overwhelm yourself. When you're sure that you will not be able to take on a project, learn the art of saying no immediately. The more you delay, the harder it will be to decline the request. If you are uncertain and need time to think it through, you can say, "That sounds like a great project, I'd love to help but let me check my availability and get back to you soon." Reminding ourselves of our priorities includes the precept of *delegate, delegate, delegate.* Delegating is a common and essential practice in the workplace and the church. When you delegate, you have found the best way to spread out the work to increase productivity. Delegating means that you trust your team's ability. If things don't go well, evaluate and learn from the example. Then, continue to practice the precept of delegating.

Eradicate time thieves. Time thieves come in many forms. Poor communication robs you of time because you have to continually seek the information before you can accomplish the task. An interruption can be a very subtle time thief. Interruptions waste your time and break your concentration, so you'll need more time to regain your focus. Social network addictions can also be time thieves. It is beneficial to put your social networking on the clock.

Schedule specific time for email, Facebook, and other platforms and refuse to allow social networking to be a time thief. We all have the same 24 hours in a day and keeping our focus on our purpose is a portion of the right perspective for life and ministry. When we manage our time efficiently, we maintain the right perspective and we close the door on frustration and irritation, which are negative emotions that can be related to feeling overwhelmed.

Change the Way You Look at the Situation

Once we allow a negative thought or situation to take root, it can change our perspective. When assessing a situation, taking responsibility for yourself and your reactions can immediately change your perspective. The mind can only focus on one thought at a time. Focusing on the positive, instead of the negative, is fundamental in the process of overcoming negative thinking. Therefore, we must determine to not allow negative people or situations to dictate our emotions which gives away too much of our power.

Former First Lady Michele Obama once stated, *"One of the lessons that I grew up with was to always stay true to myself and never let what somebody else say distract you from your goals.*

And so when I hear about negative and false attacks on me as a person, I really don't invest energy in that because I know who I am."[21]

> **God gives us response-ability, which is the ability to respond to negative situations in a positive way.**

We possess the ability to choose our own emotional and behavioral response to people and circumstances. Let's say you had nothing to do with the negative situation that you find yourself in. It simply happened and now you are in the midst of it! We are still responsible for our response. This is what we call our *response-ability,* our ability to respond in a positive way and we all possess this ability because of *"Christ in us the hope of glory"* (Colossians 1:27).

To respond in a positive manner, it is imperative that we train ourselves to respond, "I am responsible for myself." This is self-control or temperance, an attribute of God's Spirit (Galatians 5:23). Self-control is yielding control of our soul to the fruit produced by the Holy Spirit within us. As we make a conscious and consistent effort in our response-ability, the Holy Spirit will help us to look at things differently and maintain the right perspective.

---

[21] https://www.forbes.com/sites/francesbridges/2017/05/31/michelle-obamas-best-advice-to-young-people/#5f23cf995083. Accessed January 6, 2020.

Keep Moving Forward

The reality of life sometimes encourages us to "Accept what is, let go of what was, and have faith in your journey."[22] Sometimes it seems that we are run into one dead end after another, which may be a sign that we are not on the right path. Maybe you were meant to hang a left back when you took a right. That is perfectly fine, life gradually teaches us that U-turns are allowed.

Turn around when you must, but by any means necessary, keep moving forward! Thoughts like "from now on" or "from this moment" release us from our past mistakes and keep us moving forward when we have to change direction. The Apostle Paul declares, *"Brethren, I count not myself to have apprehended: but this one thing I do, forgetting those things which are behind, and reaching forth unto those things which are before, I press toward the mark for the prize of the high calling of God in Christ Jesus"* (Philippians 3:13-14 KJV).

By concentrating and controlling our thoughts, we forget the failures in our past and reach move forward. The life lesson or precept that Paul teaches us is that moving forward has two components: forgetting and reaching forth. The past cannot be forgotten without reaching forth to what lies ahead. Determine within yourself to hold on to what is valuable and to let go of that which is not valuable! It was cartoonist Bill Keane that once remarked, *"Yesterday is history, tomorrow is a mystery, today is a gift and that's why we call it the present."*

As I focus on the present and presence of the Lord, God reveals the clearest path to move forward because my mind

---

[22] http://www.marcandangel.com/2015/11/08/things-you-learn-as-you-let-go-of-the-uncontrollable/. Accessed December 25, 2019.

is clear of toxic thoughts of the past that becomes a gift in the present.

The Color of Our Thoughts

Have you ever really given much thought to how many colors we see throughout the course of a day? Think about playing with a kaleidoscope as a child. When you turned the kaleidoscope, you would see a new picture with different colors. Think about colors. A rainbow has a spectrum of colors. A person who is colorblind sees the rainbow, but they never see the diversity of its colors. We are colorblind to our thoughts because we cannot see them. This chapter began with a quote from the leadership of Marcus Aurelius, Roman Emperor, 161-180 A.D. *"The things you think about determine the quality of your mind. Your soul takes on the color of your thoughts."*

Let's take a look at the word soul. In its most basic sense, soul means life or breath, either physical or eternal. In the original Hebrew, the word soul is translated as *nepes*, which basically means breath.[23] In Greek, soul is translated *pusche*, or the seat of personality, the element of humanity by which we perceive, feel, and desire; our emotions or our entire being.[24] In Genesis 2:7, *"God formed man from the dust of the ground and breathed into his nostrils the breath of life; and the man became a living soul."* The relationship between mankind and God is often expressed by the soul.

---

[23] Mounce's Complete Expository Dictionary of Old and New Testament Words. Wordsearch bible Software, Version 12, 2012. Accessed January 6, 2020.

[24] https://www.biblestudytools.com/lexicons/greek/kjv/psuche.html. Accessed January 8, 2020.

David declared, "*My soul yearns for you in the night, my spirit within me earnestly seeks you. O God, you are my God, I seek you, my soul thirsts for you; my flesh faints for you*" (Psalms 63:1).

The Old and New Testaments reiterate that we are to love God completely, with the whole soul, with everything that is in us that makes us alive (Deuteronomy 6:4-5; Mark 12:30). I had never given much consideration to my soul (our emotions or being) taking on the color of my thoughts. If we are prone to having negative thoughts, then we can conclude that many of our thoughts are potentially colored very ugly. So, how does this affect our souls?

Aurelius also stated, "*The mind will take the shape of what you frequently hold in thought, for the human spirit is colored by such impressions.*"[25] Just as water takes on the pattern or shape of the cup or glass into which it is poured, Aurelius believed that our thoughts can be colored by the pattern, mold or impressions by which our thoughts are shaped.

When the soul (mind, intellect, and will) is colored with the wrong thoughts, life will be dyed the same way. For instance, although King David was a man after God's heart, he suffered terrible consequences when his mind and thoughts were shaped, patterned, and molded by the impressions of lust for Bathsheba. He spotted Bathsheba bathing while walking upon his rooftop and then summonsed her to his palace to sleep with her although she was married to Uriah, one of his soldiers. David then had Uriah killed in battle to cover his sins (1 Samuel 13:14; 2 Samuel 11:2; 2 Samuel 23:39). The color of David's thoughts and soul was the catalyst for his sin.

---

[25] https://dailystoic.com/meditations-marcus-aurelius/. Accessed January 6, 2020.

A precept or life lesson that we learn from David is that if we allow our soul to be in control, then our soul will negatively influence our thoughts. In turn, negative thoughts will color our actions and conduct with potentially devastating consequences.

It is also important to note that David repented and declared, *"Create in me a new, clean heart, O God, filled with clean thoughts and right desires"* (Psalm 51:10, TLB). At this point, the color of David's thoughts and the pattern of his thinking were reshaped by repentance and accountability so that he was brought back to the attributes of quality thinking.

How to Manage the Color of Your Thoughts

The human brain, partnered with the mind, is an incredible organ capable of making imaginative leaps, recalling memories, and finding insights at a moment's notice, and science has proven that we will never be able to control every thought.[26] A better method is to be aware of our thoughts as they come and go. For example, if you are told not to think about a banana, your mind is automatically going to think about a banana!

Thinking about ignoring the banana, paradoxically, never works. Therefore, what we are suggesting is that we can improve the quality of our thoughts, which assists us in the process of managing the color of our thoughts that influences our emotions and perceptions (the soul).

---

[26] https://www.iflscience.com/brain/new-research-suggests-we-have-no-control-over-our-thoughts/. Accessed December 25, 2019.

Choose friends wisely. The quality of our thoughts affects the decisions that we make, and our decisions determine the quality of our lives. The thoughts you expose yourself to will unavoidably influence or color the way that you think so you must be careful about who and what you allow into your mind. Choose friends with discretion because they have the potential to influence and shape the way that you think. The people you friend, follow, and like on social media are also important to consider. Some thoughts on social media are good and helpful while others are negative and potentially detrimental to the quality of our thinking.

Avoid responding to negative external factors. The way we think also manifests in our actions. If our mind is always filled with jumbled, chaotic thoughts, then our output will be jumbled and chaotic. Instead of enjoying evenings at home with our families, our thoughts can be centered on some aspect of work instead of investing love, attention, and affection in the lives of our spouse and children. The quality of our thoughts also reflects our values. When we are clear on what is important to us, it becomes easier to block out negative thoughts and distractions that impede us from becoming better people. We should focus on what we can control and avoid external factors that we cannot influence.

We may not get to decide who gets the next promotion in the company, but you can support your co-worker in their new position as a member of the team. You can't force a person with a bad attitude to change his or her demeanor, but you can respond in a kind and friendly manner.

Your quality thoughts and subsequent actions have the potential to influence others to do the same.

Direct your thoughts instead of reacting to negative thoughts. If we direct our thoughts, then we will not react to contrary thoughts. Consider destructive, negative thoughts as a car hydroplaning and sliding out of control. Instinctively, your mind (thoughts) governs your body's reactions. You begin to pump the car's brakes and turn the steering wheel in the direction that you believe will correct the vehicle. An instinct is a way of behaving, thinking, or feeling that is not learned.[27] Instinct causes us to act in a particular way without thinking about it, a natural God-given ability. As we become proficient in what God has placed inside of us, we become more proficient at directing our thoughts instinctively.

Pay attention to your thought patterns and take every negative thought captive (2 Corinthians 10:5). Additionally, watch your vocabulary or what you say out loud. For example, comments such as "I'll never be able to do this!" or "I am always messing up!" result from negative thinking. If you constantly hear the same negative thought patterns, it is time to arrest those thoughts! Don't beat yourself up for thinking negative thoughts because this just continues the cycle. We cannot stop negative thoughts passing through our minds, but we can reduce the intensity of the thoughts by remaining attentive to them as they arise.

Know your rights. A thief is a criminal and we must refuse to be robbed by negative thoughts that keep us from God's plan for our lives. Negative thoughts have no authority in our lives! By the warranty and authority of the mind of Christ (quality thoughts), we gain or regain control of our thoughts.

---

[27] https://www.vocabulary.com/dictionary/instinct. Accessed January 6, 2020.

Aristotle stated, *"The mark of an educated mind is to be able to entertain a thought without accepting it."*[28] In other words, we don't have to accept a negative thought. We change the station to another thought that is acceptable. Yes, you have the right to replace bad thoughts with good ones! If a negative thought says, "I am not good enough," then it is your legal right to rebut with *"I am God's workmanship and I am created in Christ Jesus to do good works and God ordained this in the beginning!"* (Ephesians 2:10).

Consider how your thoughts make you feel. Feelings are connected to the soul. If your thoughts lead you to feelings of anger, worry, jealousy, disputes, envying, impurity, immorality, depression, anxiety, or strife, then they are distractions that you have a right to disregard and shut down. Thoughts that make you feel love, joy, peace, patience, kindness, goodness, faithfulness, gentleness, or self-control are quality thoughts because they develop the character of Christ in you (Galatians 5:22-23). Our thoughts, or more specifically a practiced determination to think quality thoughts, become the Crayola crayons that color our soul and help us to think like God thinks with the mind of the Lord Jesus Christ.

Having quality thoughts is the same as having the mind of Christ. Let's revisit Philippians 2:5: *"In your relationships with one another, have the same mindset as Christ Jesus..."* (NIV). Having the mind of Christ means we look at life from our Savior's point of view with His values and desires in mind. When we have the mind of Christ, we think like God thinks and not like the world. It is a shared perspective of humility, compassion, and dependence on God.

---

[28] https://philosiblog.com/2012/03/07/it-is-the-mark-of-an-educated-mind-to-be-able-to-entertain-a-thought-without-. Accessed January 6, 2020.

Principles and Precepts For
Transforming Our Thinking

"And do not be conformed to this world [any longer with its superficial values and customs], but be transformed and progressively changed [as you mature spiritually] by the renewing of your mind [focusing on godly values and ethical attitudes], so that you may prove [for yourselves] what the will of God is, that which is good and acceptable and perfect [in His plan and purpose for you]" (Romans 12:2, AMP).

Principle-a universal law that is true in any context, situation, or environment.

Precept-life lessons indicating the way one should act or behave.

Practice-the act of rehearsing a behavior over and over, for the purpose of improving or mastering it.

<u>Chapter 2 Reflection Practices</u>

1. Think of an experience where you reacted with a perspective that did not align with God's view.

    What principles and precepts from this chapter can you use to respond differently?

2. Use the scale outlined below to rate your *response-ability*. Then, look for opportunities this week to apply at least two principles and precepts to negative situations.

o The scale ranges from 1 to 5.

o 1 means "I always respond to negative situations in a negative manner."

o 2 means "I frequently respond to negative situations in a negative manner."

o 3 means "I sometimes respond to negative situations in a negative manner."

o 4 means "I don't usually respond to negative situations in a negative manner."

o 5 means "I never respond to negative situations in a negative manner."

3. Begin each day this week with the things that matter most. Study the techniques given in this chapter and create a schedule that allows you opportunity to start each day using the recommendations given.

Chapter 3

THINKING LIKE GOD
THINKS CRUSHES FEAR

When we train ourselves to think like God thinks, we develop the capability to crush all of our fears. Merriam Webster's Dictionary defines crush as "to break something into powder or very small pieces by pressing, pounding, or grinding it; to defeat a person or group that opposes you by the use of force."

In addition, "crushing it" is a common modern-day expression used when someone is doing a task or assignment well or exceeding all of their goals. To "crush it" also means "to accomplish" according to the Urban Dictionary.

The Modern English translation of Matthew 11:12 says, *"From the days of John the Baptist until now, the kingdom of heaven has forcefully advanced, and the strong take it by force."* In the larger context of this passage, Jesus is pointing to the huge crowds that followed John and were now following Him. Jesus likens the crowd to an invading army surrounding a city to capture it. In other words, from the time John the Baptist preached of Jesus, there has been a great multitude of people pressing in from everywhere craving for the blessing of the kingdom. The phrase *"kingdom of heaven has forcefully advanced"* figuratively compares the multitude that had gathered to hear the gospel to an army trying to lay siege to a city. The *"strong take it by force"* does not mean that the people entering the kingdom were violent.

Instead, their eagerness to see the coming of the Messiah was so overwhelming that it was as if they were attacking the city and beating down the doors to enter!

The suggestion is that the people were not afraid, but rather they were strong, and they made the decision to disregard obstacles and move forward to obtain the promise of the kingdom. Fear is a strategy of the enemy designed to keep us from advancing the kingdom of God in the earth and in our lives. Therefore, it is vital that as God's people we crush our fears, defeating whatever opposes us by thinking like God thinks. This chapter includes five precepts that can help us to crush fear:

o   The Reality of Fear
o   God Has Not Given Us the Spirit of Fear
o   Paul: A Biblical Example of "Crushing It"
o   Perfect Love Casts Out Fear
o   Additional Weapons from the Word to Combat Fear

The Reality of Fear

Fear is a powerful human emotion that alerts us to the presence of danger.

When we confront a perceived threat, our bodies respond in specific ways. Physical reactions to fear include sweating, increased heart rate, and high adrenaline levels that make us extremely alert in what has been called the "fight or flight" response.[29] Emotions are simply a normal part of the human experience. As such, emotions are neither good or bad. The field of affective science has concluded that fear and anxiety are actually particularly important emotions. When it comes to human survival and achievement, anxiety and fear actually motivate us to take necessary action.[30] The science of fear reveals that some fears may be a result of experiences or trauma, while others may represent a fear of something else entirely, such as a loss of control.

Other fears may occur because they cause physical symptoms, such as being afraid of heights because they make you feel dizzy and sick to your stomach. Scientists are trying to understand exactly what fear is and what causes it, but this is a supremely difficult undertaking in light of the differences between individuals in terms of what they fear and why.[31] According to the Mental Help website, fear is a response to an immediate danger in the present moment of time, while anxiety is associated with a threat that is anticipated in a future moment of time.[32] The word fear itself originates in the Greek *phobos*, which may be translated as terror, dread or intimidation.

Our English word phobia originates from *phobos*.[33] There are many types of phobias. Social phobias involve the fear of

---

[29] https://www.verywellmind.com/the-psychology-of-fear-2671696. Accessed November 17, 2019

[30] https://en.wikipedia.org/wiki/Affective_science. Accessed November 17, 2019.

[31] Ibid, November 17, 2019.

[32] https://www.mentalhelp.net/anxiety/normal-and-abnormal-whats-the-difference/. Accessed November 17, 2019

[33] https://www.biblestudytools.com/dictionary/fear/. Accessed January 10, 2020.

people, which often include anxiety disorders and excessive self-consciousness in social situations. Some people can fear being judged so much that they avoid specific situations, like eating in front of others. This type of fear can then potentially segue into a fear of rejection. Rejection knows no bounds. It invades relationships with family, neighbors, and co-workers because the person constantly feels that they're not wanted or valued. Another very powerful fear is the fear of failure, which can be linked to having critical or unsupportive parents.[34] Fear of failure can also be caused by experiencing a traumatic event. For example, a person may have a terrible experience where they did very poorly on an important presentation in front of a large group. The experience might have been so terrible that they are now afraid of failing in other things years later.[35]

The list of phobias can literally go from A to Z! Take a look at these phobias.

o   Pogonophobia- fear of beards
o   Somniphobia- fear of falling asleep
o   Coulrophobia – fear of clowns
o   Nomophobia- fear of being without mobile phone coverage
o   Ombrophobia- fear of rain
o   Achievemephobia- fear of success [36]

---

[34] https://news.stanford.edu/news/2013/september/anxiety-disorder-therapy-090413.html. Accessed January 10, 2020.
[35] https://www.mindtools.com/pages/article/fear-of-failure.htm. Accessed January 10, 2020.
[36] https://www.fearof.net/fear-of-success-phobia-achievemephobia/. Accessed January 10, 2020.

Fear is an enormously powerful emotion! The preceding examples are all very real for many. However, they can all be overcome by thinking like God thinks.

God Has Not Given Us the Spirit of Fear

The reality is that fear exists and that it can be healthy or unhealthy. Fear is not necessarily a bad thing.

It is one of the God-given, inbuilt human survival instincts that helps to protect us, which is healthy. Fear that paralyzes action is unhealthy. This is the spirit of fear, from Satan, that is designed to keep us shackled in bondage. The Amplified Version of 2 Timothy 1:7 proclaims, *"For God did not give us a spirit of timidity or cowardice or fear, but [He has given us a spirit] of power and of love and of sound judgment and personal discipline [abilities that result in a calm, well-balanced mind and self-control]."* No matter what fears we face, we can crush and overcome them! Determination to succeed, persevere, and move forward necessitates using force to crush the unhealthy fears that oppose us.

> *When we apply God's Word that is borne of His Spirit, it will crush the influence of our unhealthy fears.*

Our battle against demonically influenced fear is not a physical one, it is spiritual. This is an example where we can take the spiritual, make it practical, so that it becomes natural to live spiritual!

Look at the words that Zechariah recorded about Zerubbabel: *"It is not by force nor by strength, but by my Spirit, says the* LORD *of Heaven's Armies. Nothing, not even a mighty mountain, will stand in Zerubbabel's way; it will become a level plain before him"* (Zechariah 4:6-7, NLT). We crush unhealthy fear by the Spirit of the Living God! When we apply His Word that is borne of His Spirit, it will crush the influence of our unhealthy fears! As we practice overcoming negative thoughts, there are several techniques that we can use to crush and defeat unhealthy fear.

Identify your choices and options*.* Analyze (but don't overanalyze) your choices and evaluate your best course of action concerning the negative thought or experience.

Seek external perspectives and fresh points of view from the Word, trust God, take aim, and take action. *"And your ears shall hear a word behind you, saying, 'This is the way, walk in it,' when you turn to the right or when you turn to the left"* (Isaiah 30:21, ESV).

> *"You can't attack the giants in your life if you are not aiming to strike and hit the target. You can't run a race in vain if you have no plans to win or finish it. Start, strive and aim high…never give up. Your best is yet to come!"* — Kemi Sogunle

Accept and understand*.* What is the driving force behind your fear? Who is in the driver's seat, you or your fear? What is the foundation of this particular fear? What is the root cause? What triggers the fear? With practice, unhealthy fear can be controlled by the wisdom of God's Word.

"Make your ear attentive to wisdom and incline your heart to understanding; yes, if you call out for insight and raise your voice for understanding if you seek it like silver and search for it as for hidden treasures, then you will understand the fear (reverence) of the LORD *and find the knowledge of God"* (Proverbs 2:2-5, ESV).

Remove the barriers. Fear builds barriers that can hold us back from achieving our life assignments in accordance with God's plan. Take a moment to examine any real or imagined barriers. Barriers may include anxiety, inaction, need for control, defensiveness, fearing you can't do it, and being comfortable with the way things are.

Other barriers include distrust, suspicion, exhaustion, paralysis, instant gratification, lack of confidence, impatience, and a need for safety and security. Identifying the major barriers holding you back and creating and taking daily action steps is the path to crushing and defeating our barriers.

"Do not be anxious about anything, but in everything, by prayer and petition, with thanksgiving, present your requests to God. And the peace of God, which transcends all understanding, will guard your hearts and your minds in Christ Jesus" (Philippians 4:6-7).

"There are no constraints on the human mind, no walls around the human spirit, no barriers to our progress except those we ourselves erect." -Ronald Reagan

Paul: A Biblical Example of *Crushing It*

Now, we will analyze Paul's experiences to gain more techniques to combat fear.

Realize that God is with you. In the Amplified Version of Acts 18:9-10, the Bible records, *"And one night the Lord said to Paul in a vision, have no fear, but speak and do not keep silent. For I am with you, and no man shall assault you to harm you, for I have many people in this city."*

Paul speaks of his fear in 1 Corinthians 2:3, *"I came to you in weakness and fear, and with much trembling."* Additional study suggests that Paul sensed a deep personal inadequacy before the Corinthians because they stressed eloquence and charisma in speakers (1 Cor. 2:4; 2 Cor. 10:10; 2 Cor. 11:6). Apostle Paul was a great man and leader, but he also had to overcome his negative thoughts and possible fear of rejection. Paul was able to crush this fear because he knew that the Lord was with him! Paul's strength to overcome was in God.

Acknowledge weakness. Paul learned to endure adversity and boast in his weaknesses.

> *"I have been in prison frequently, been flogged ...severely, and been exposed to death again and again. Five times I received from the Jews the forty lashes minus one. Three times I was beaten with rods, once I was stoned, three times I was shipwrecked. I spent a night and a day in the open sea, I have been constantly on the move.*
>
> *I have been in danger from rivers, in danger from bandits, in danger from my own countrymen, in*

danger from Gentiles; in danger in the city, in danger in the country, in danger at sea; and in danger from false brothers. ...I have known hunger and thirst and have often gone without food; I have been cold and naked....Who is weak, and I do not feel weak? Who is led into sin, and I do not inwardly burn? If I must boast, I will boast of the things that show my weakness." (2 Corinthians 11:23-30, NIV)

Paul also acknowledged His weaknesses before the Lord, which caused the power of God to rest on him. He records his experience in 2 Corinthians 12:7-10, CEB:

"I was given a thorn in my body because of the outstanding revelations I've received so that I wouldn't be conceited.

It's a messenger from Satan sent to torment me so that I wouldn't be conceited. I pleaded with the Lord three times for it to leave me alone. He said to me, "My grace is enough for you, because power is made perfect in weakness." So, I'll gladly spend my time bragging about my weaknesses so that Christ's power can rest on me. Therefore, I'm all right with weaknesses, insults, disasters, harassments, and stressful situations for the sake of Christ, because when I'm weak, then I'm strong."

God wanted Paul to understand that His grace was enough for him. In other words, God's presence, love, favor, and blessings are enough to help the believer walk through any suffering and hardship that are undoubtedly accompanied persistently by negative thoughts. Paul also learned that the power of Christ is made perfect in his weakness.

The word perfect in this passage means finished, and complete; fully grown, or mature.[37] Perfect does not mean without flaw. Through these experiences, Paul became an example of a believer that acquired the ability to crush his fears because he realized that God's help becomes most potent when he acknowledged his flaws and asked for help.

> *When we acknowledge our weaknesses, we affirm God's strength!*

In other words, Paul is saying that he is being developed and he is satisfied by the grace and the will of God for his life simply because the grace of God rests upon him and covers his life like a tent in his weaknesses, empowering him and enabling him to overcome negative thoughts and experiences!

Our weaknesses not only help develop Christian character, they also deepen our worship because in admitting our weakness, we affirm God's strength. On the other hand, when we believe that we are strong in our own abilities or resources, we are tempted to rely on our own understanding, which leads to pride. When we are weak and we allow God's power to rest over us like a tent, we become stronger than we could ever be on our own. When we are weak and allow God's power to rest upon us, we become stronger than we ever could be on our own!

---

[37] Vine's Expository Dictionary of Old Testament and New Testament Words, Wordsearch 12 Software. Accessed January 10, 2020.

We must depend on God's power and grace because they are forces that help us to grind, pound, and ultimately crush our fears so that we can think like God thinks. We will conclude this section by substantiating the lessons we learned from Paul with some words of wisdom from Former First Lady Eleanor Roosevelt illustrating the development and capability of crushing fear.

> *"You gain strength, courage and confidence by every experience in which you really stop to look fear in the face. You are able to say to yourself, 'I have lived through this horror. I can take the next thing that comes along.' You must do the thing you think you cannot do."*

Perfect Love Casts Out All Fear

Jesus asks His followers in Mark 4:40, *"Why are ye so fearful? how is it that ye have no faith?"* The Bible also tells us that *"There is no fear in love, but perfect love drives out fear, because fear expects punishment. The person who is afraid has not been made perfect in love"* 1 John 4:18 (CEB). Fear carries torment. Fear thinks about and expects punishment, suffering or loss. It causes all kinds of unpleasant emotions, phobias, neurosis, and even more serious psychotic disorders. The torment of fear is one of the worst problems faced by man. God offers that fear means that a person is not perfected in love.

What Is Perfected Love?

Perfected love is trust in love because God is love! Perfect or mature love casts out fear. This is critical to note, for only a love that is growing, and maturing will be blessed by God. A believer cannot love one person and hold ill feelings against another. This is not love. A person who really loves, loves everyone! There is no such thing as a heart filled with love and hate. The two are incompatible. Therefore, the believer who knows the peace and assurance of God is the believer who is being perfected (matured) in love. Examine Matthew 5:43–47 in the Message Bible:

"You're familiar with the old written law, 'Love your friend,' and its unwritten companion, 'Hate your enemy.' I'm challenging that. I'm telling you to love your enemies. Let them bring out the best in you, not the worst. When someone gives you a hard time, respond with the energies of prayer, for then you are working out of your true selves, your God-created selves. This is what God does. He gives his best—the sun to warm and the rain to nourish—to everyone, regardless: the good and bad, the nice and nasty. If all you do is love the lovable, do you expect a bonus? Anybody can do that. If you simply say hello to those who greet you, do you expect a medal? Any run-of-the-mill sinner does that. In a word, what I'm saying is, Grow up. You're kingdom subjects. Now live like it. Live out your God-created identity. Live generously and graciously toward others, the way God lives toward you."

Perfected love forgives. It does not matter what anyone has said about us or done to us, perfect love loves like God loves. God's love includes forgiveness without bound.

When a Christian does not forgive, it becomes inconsistent with the infinite forgiveness of God. It is important to note that forgiveness is not a feeling; it is a choice. Choosing forgiveness sometimes means that you have to go to God on your knees for the power to forgive. It's choosing not to let negative thoughts of others rule in your heart. It's choosing to go to God to find help and comfort instead of dwelling on the past, even when our emotions would rather do anything but forgive. Does forgiving negate the pain you have suffered? Does it reverse the things that have happened to you? Does it mean the person who wronged you doesn't have to take responsibility for his or her actions? No, but you will be free from the thoughts of the anger and bitterness of the incident. When you know that it is not in you to forgive, then you have to find it in Christ because you can *"do all things through Christ who strengthens you"* (Philippians 4:13). Forgiveness is not only done for the sake of the one you are forgiving, but for your own sake so that you don't have to live with the negative thoughts of unforgiveness.

Perfect love starts with God. The way that God lives towards all of us is the way of love. A biblical definition of love starts with God, never with us (1 John 4:9-10). God is love personified and it is His character that defines love. The pure and perfect love of God is typified in the love relationship between God the Father and God the Son. Jesus shows this relationship to his disciples in John 17:26.

The Passion translation reads, *"I have revealed to them who you are and I will continue to make you even more real to them, so that they may experience the same endless love that you have for me, for your love will now live in them, even as I live in them!"* The Voice translation of 1 John 4:7-8 says, *"My loved ones, let us devote ourselves to loving one another. Love comes straight from*

God, and everyone who loves is born of God and truly knows God. Anyone who does not love does not know God, because God is love."

Perfect love that drives out fear is the Message Bible version of Matthew 3:17 where God the Father says to Jesus, *"This is my Son, chosen and marked by my love, the delight of my life."* The Phillips New Testament translation of Ephesians 1:6 declares, *"He planned, in His purpose of love, that we should be adopted as his own children through Jesus Christ—that we might learn to praise that glorious generosity of His which has made us welcome in the everlasting love he bears towards the Son."* Knowing that we have been adopted into the family of God through Jesus Christ and that He has made us welcome in His everlasting love reminds us that we don't have to fear because His love is perfect!

Additional Weapons from the Word to Combat Fear

Perfect love is a powerful weapon. A soldier never enters a place of battle without his or her weapons for the fight. God's Word also provides us with an untold number of weapons to fight on the battlefield of our minds. The Phillips New Testament translates 2 Corinthians 10:3-4 as, *"the truth is that, although of course, we lead normal human lives, the battle we are fighting is on the spiritual level.*

The very weapons we use are not those of human warfare but powerful in God's warfare for the destruction of the enemy's strongholds." This passage is designed to stir believers to discipline so that we gain control over our minds and thoughts. It is a reminder that there is a battle going on, and the battle is in our mind where we must combat and destroy the stronghold of fear. Here are some additional passages that will help you fight fear:

Acknowledge that God is on your side. *"He will never leave you nor forsake you. Do not be afraid; do not be discouraged"* (Deuteronomy 31:8). *"Don't fear, for I have redeemed you; I have called you by name; you are Mine"* (Isaiah 43:1). God actually commands us not to fear or worry! When you're afraid of a situation or you experience some emotional challenge, hear God speaking these scriptures to you.

Know your authority in God's sovereignty. *"Have not I commanded thee? Be strong and of a good courage; be not afraid, neither be thou dismayed: for the LORD thy God is with thee whithersoever thou goest"* (Joshua 1:9). The people's hearts were gripped with a deep sense of grief and anguish, broken over the passing of Moses who was the Father of the nation of Israel. It was time for Joshua to arise and cease his mourning over the death of Moses. It was time for him to take up the mantle of leadership and lead God's people into their inheritance in the Promised Land. It was now Joshua's duty. As it was for Joshua, so it is for you and me. We must overcome the pain of yesterday, rise and fulfill our duty, and answer God's calling to His people!

God is with you in the worst times. *"Yea, though I walk through the valley of the shadow of death, I will fear no evil: for thou art with me; thy rod and thy staff they comfort me"* (Psalms 23:4). Valleys are symbols of the darkest times of life. The valley of the shadow of death speaks of life's gravest circumstances with fearful occasions that threaten to destroy us.

No illness or disease (including the coronavirus), criminal assault or attack, or bad doctor's report can overshadow God's presence.

Know that God hears you and refuse to worry. *"I sought the Lord, and he heard me, and delivered me from all my fears"* (Psalms 34:4). David experienced a number of terrors in his young life: a lion, a bear, and a giant by the name of Goliath. When King Saul pursued him in jealousy, David was gripped by fear so he sought the Lord, asking Him for His protection. In every case, God heard and answered David by giving him strength and guidance, delivering him from all of his fears! He will do the same for us now!

Receive God's peace. *"Peace I leave with you, my peace I give unto you: not as the world giveth, give I unto you. Let not your heart be troubled, neither let it be afraid"* (John 14:27). When we believe in Jesus and know that He is the Son of God, we can receive His peace.

His peace means experiencing the highest good, enjoying the absolute best life possible. God's peace keeps us from being afraid!

> *"This battle is not for you to fight; take your position, stand still, and see the victory of the LORD on your behalf, O Judah and Jerusalem.' Do not fear or be dismayed; tomorrow go out against them, and the LORD will be with you."* (2 Chronicles 20:17, NRSV)

When we train ourselves to believe God and think like He thinks, we develop the ability to crush all of our fears.

Principles and Precepts For
Transforming Our Thinking

"And do not be conformed to this world [any longer with its superficial values and customs], but be transformed and progressively changed [as you mature spiritually] by the renewing of your mind [focusing on godly values and ethical attitudes]

So that you may prove [for yourselves] what the will of God is, that which is good and acceptable and perfect [in His plan and purpose for you]" (Romans 12:2, AMP).

Principle-a universal law that is true in any context, situation, or environment.

Precept-life lessons indicating the way one should act or behave.

Practice-the act of rehearsing a behavior over and over, for the purpose of improving or mastering it.

Chapter 3 Reflection Practices

1. Fear can be healthy or unhealthy. Review the difference between the two as discussed in this chapter.

   o What does God call unhealthy fear? (2 Timothy 1:7)
   o Think of a situation where you displayed healthy fear. Then, think of an experience with unhealthy fear.
   o What other scriptures can you use to combat unhealthy fears?

2. Paul realized that it was good to acknowledge his weaknesses before the Lord. Spend approximately 15 minutes discussing your weaknesses with God.

   o Why is it important to acknowledge your weaknesses before God?
   o Take a portion of the 15 minutes to ask God to help you with your weaknesses.

Chapter 4

THE FAITH FACTOR AND WHAT WE THINK

"Have faith in God." – Jesus

The pages of James' epistle are filled with direct commands to pursue a life of trust and obedience. He makes no excuses for those who do not measure up. In the mind of this early church leader, a faith that does not partner with action is incomplete. Consider James 2:22-24 in the New Living Translation:

> *"You see, his faith and his actions worked together. His actions made his faith complete. And so it happened just as the Scriptures say: "Abraham believed God, and God counted him as righteous because of his faith." He was even called the friend of God. So you see, we are shown to be right with God by what we do, not by faith alone."*

In this chapter we will examine the faith of Abraham and use the concepts to develop our skills to think like God thinks. We all think differently. Have you ever wondered why you, your spouse, family members, co-workers or friends think differently about the same concept?

No matter how differently we may think, everyone has faith in something that they don't consciously think about! We have an unconscious faith that when we place the key in the ignition of our car that the engine is going to start. We have an unconscious faith that when we place our money in the bank that it will be there when we are ready to make a withdrawal. We simply believe without really thinking about it. This is an unmindful, inattentive, and unconscious faith. When we think like God thinks, we must have a mindful, attentive, and conscious faith in God.

James' usage of the word faith denotes both an act and a possession of the thing believed. This kind of faith is mindful, attentive, and conscious even when the desired goal cannot be seen. With this faith, the goal is real and existing, and we can possess it by believing and having faith. Faith trusts and possesses all that God is and says. Faith is confident and possesses all that God is and says.

Faith hopes for and possesses because God exists and has promised it. Just like Abraham, when our faith and actions work together, our actions complete our faith. This is what we will call the *faith factor*. A factor contributes to the production of a particular result. Faith and action in God contribute to successfully overcoming negative thinking.

> *The faith factor, which is the collaboration of faith and actions, gives us power to overcome negative thinking.*

Faith and Action Defeat Negative Thinking

From James' perspective, faith and action have formed a partnership. A partner does his or her part in a collaborative effort towards accomplishing a task or completing an assignment. Exceptional partnerships create a synergy and energy collaboratively to the success of the whole.

The word complete originates from the Latin *completum* which means "to reach a state of fullness in such a way that none of its parts are missing, to make whole or perfect."[38] James declares, *"Faith by itself isn't enough. Unless it produces good deeds, it is dead and useless"* (James 2: 17 – 18). In other words, our actions complete faith.

God gave me a powerful life lesson on how action is required to overcome negative thinking towards others. I can remember many years ago walking in downtown Milwaukee, Wisconsin. I had preached at a conference with several hundred people in attendance and I thought I was full of faith. There was a homeless man sitting to the left of me that I paid no attention to. However, when I got a few feet past this

---

[38] https://www.etymonline.com/word/complete. Accessed January 11, 2020.

homeless man, I heard the voice of the Lord say, "That could be you." God taught me a great lesson of ministry that day.

Although I had seen the man, I really had not seen the man. I was only focused on myself and not on the purpose of the Lord to be a witness of His love and grace. I had faith, but God wanted me to know that faith and actions must collaborate. Even though I had not necessarily thought negatively about the man, *my attitude was worse!* I didn't think about the man at all! Overcoming negative thinking might involve overcoming an attitude of indifference. The nature of indifference itself is negative because it is a lack of care, concern, or interest. We overcome an attitude of indifference by developing and cultivating an attitude of gratitude by being givers. People with an attitude of gratitude are motivated and inspired by the nature of Psalm 103:2 (NLT), *"Let all that I am praise the LORD; may I never forget the good things he does for me."* Consider the statement, "She has an attitude!" Our thought concerning this statement maybe that she is disagreeable, or has a negative outlook on a topic, thing, or person.

But what about the other side of attitude? There is a positive side that moves us in the right direction. Micah 6:8 tells us, *"Do justly, (what is right) love mercy and walk humbly before thy God."* God taught me on the streets of Milwaukee that I needed to shift my negative thinking (*attitude of indifference*) into an attitude of gratitude by combining faith with action. A lesson that I am still learning to practice today!

What exactly is faith? Before we can partner our faith with action, we need to discuss biblical faith and look at how the Bible defines faith. I believe this is the clearest definition of biblical faith. *"Faith is the assurance of things hoped for, the conviction of things not seen"* (Hebrews 11:1, ESV). What gives us assurance? If you buy a lottery ticket, of course you hope that you win the lottery.

That is why you bought the ticket! However, you do not have assurance that you will win.

You have no way of knowing that your ticket is any better than the millions of other lottery tickets out there competing for the same pot.

If you had x-ray vision, and you could see through the grey scratch-off coating on the lottery tickets, then you would know if you had the $30 million-dollar winner. In that case, you no longer just hope that you win, you have an assurance because you have seen the winning number. When we have this type of assurance in God (even when we cannot see the objective), it is easier to act.

According to the Amplified version of Hebrews 12:2, God is the source of our faith. *"Looking away [from all that will distract] to Jesus, Who is the Leader and the Source of our faith [giving the first incentive for our belief] and is also its Finisher [bringing it to maturity and perfection]."* Since God is the source and originator of our faith, we can ask Him for faith and then couple this faith with action. Let's look at an acronym to concisely define faith that involves action.

Faith is

- Forward
- Action
- In
- Trusting
- Him

Note that this acronym highlights the faith factor, the collaboration of faith and action. We execute the faith factor when we move to prepare for the future (forward) by taking the initiative and working (action) with confidence and resting in our minds on the integrity and veracity (in trusting) of Jesus Christ (Him)!

What Is action? We now have an understanding of faith, but how do we take action? How do we take the initiative? How do we work? How do we act? In fact, what is action?

Action is

- *A*ctivated
- *C*onfidence
- *T*riumphant
- *I*n
- *O*vercoming
- *N*egativity

A call to action means that we come alive, we are animated (activated) with certainty (confidence) that we will be victorious and notably successful (triumphant) in consistently gaining the superiority over (overcoming) opposition, resistance, pessimism, or bad thinking (negativity). The two acronyms show how the partnership of faith and action create a firm coalition and alliance to defeat negative thinking.

> *The partnership of faith and action create a firm coalition and alliance to defeat negative thinking.*

The Faith Factor: How Should You Think to Win?

Realize that you have to fight. Even with faith and action as our allies, overcoming negative thinking will not occur without a fight! Paul tells Timothy to *"fight the good fight of faith...."* (**1 Timothy 6:12**). Fight means to "agonize, struggle, battle, contend, and fight for the prize." Fight carries the connotation of a desperate effort and struggle. However, Jesus reminds us that the fight to overcome negative thinking is fixed and that He has already won the fight for us!

> *"I have told you these things, so that in Me you may have [perfect] peace and confidence. In the world you have tribulation and trials and distress and frustration; but be of good cheer [take courage; be confident, certain, undaunted]! For I have overcome the world. [I have deprived it of power to harm you and have conquered it for you."* (John 16:33, AMP)

Our spiritual weapons will crush the enemy! Paul announces that there are weapons available to help us fight and they are very powerful.

> *"God is strong, and he wants you strong. Take everything the Master has set out for you, well-made weapons of the best materials. And put them to use so you will be able to stand up to everything the devil throws your way. This is no afternoon athletic contest that we'll walk away from and forget about in a couple of hours. This is for keeps, a life-or-death fight to the finish against the devil and all his angels. Be prepared. You're up against far more than you can*

> *handle on your own. Take all the help you can get,*
> *every weapon God has issued, so that when it's all*
> *over but the shouting you'll still be on your feet.*
>
> *Truth, righteousness, peace, faith, and salvation are*
> *more than words. Learn how to apply them. You'll*
> *need them throughout your life. God's Word is an*
> *indispensable weapon."* (Ephesians 6:10-17, MSG)

Paul is saying that being clothed in the armor of God makes us have activated, confident triumph in overcoming negativity. The faith factor (faith and action in collaboration) empowered by the armor of God guarantees the believer a sure victory in overcoming negative thinking.

What Was Abraham Thinking?

In the primary text for this chapter, James reports that Abraham's faith and actions worked together (James 2:22-24). Let's look at Abraham's model. God told Abram to leave his country and go to another land where he would make him a great nation, bless him, make his name great, and cause him to be a blessing (Genesis 12:1-3).

I believe that most of us would agree that Abram was undoubtedly thinking about his future. However, it took almost 25 years for his faith to be counted as righteousness (Genesis 15:6). Abraham believed God although His promises appeared to be impossible. I am wondering, "What was Abraham thinking during his journey to fulfil the promise?"

Abraham Got Discouraged

Righteousness, in the original Hebrew, is a legal term which involves the whole process of justice. Righteousness further means, "to be in the right, to be justified, be just."[39] For God's people, righteousness means to pattern our lives after Him. Abraham's thoughts may not have been completely righteous and certainly there was room for negative thoughts during his wait! Abraham laments the following:

> "O Sovereign LORD, what good are all your blessings when I don't even have a son?
>
> Since you've given me no children, Eliezer of Damascus, a servant in my household, will inherit all my wealth. You have given me no descendants of my own, so one of my servants will be my heir." (Genesis 15: 2-4)

Abraham's words were governed by his mind and thoughts. God's promises had not been fulfilled for 25 years and this caused a strain on his thinking. Abram was disappointed and discouraged to the point that he feared that he would not have a child. How did Abraham overcome this negative thinking?

Abraham Allowed God to Speak to Him

God visited Abraham in a dream and encouraged Abraham in his disappointment.

---

[39] https://www.vocabulary.com/dictionary/righteous. Accessed January 11, 2020.

> *"The* LORD *spoke to Abram in a vision and said to him, Do not be afraid, Abram, for I will protect you, and your reward will be great.*
>
> *Then the* LORD *said to him, No, your servant will not be your heir, for you will have a son of your own who will be your heir. Then the* LORD *took Abram outside and said to him, Look up into the sky and count the stars if you can. That's how many descendants you will have!"* (Genesis 15:5-7, NLT)

Now, note what God did. God gave Abraham a vision. He took him from his tent and told him to look up and count the stars. God then affirmed that Abraham's seed (descendants) would number as the stars of the sky. What a magnificent moment of encouragement! From that point on, every time Abraham looked up at the stars, he would think of the great promise of God and be encouraged and strengthened in his faith. Just imagine this moment within the vision. God caused an activation in Abraham's mind; He caused his mind to come alive again. Abraham became reassured of God's promises.

Abraham Believed God

It is important to note that this is the first time the word believe is used in Scripture is Genesis 15:6. *"Abram believed in the Lord; and He counted it to him for righteousness."* The Hebrew translation of believe actually means "amen, it will be so; it is so."[40] To believe further means to rest upon, to lean upon,

---

[40] Mounces Complete Dictionary of Old and New Testament Words. Wordsearch Bible, Version 12, 2012. Accessed January 11, 2020.

to be sure of, to have complete and full confidence in. When a person truly believes God, He takes that person's faith and counts it as righteousness. Count is an accounting term. In other words, when Abraham deposited his faith in God, God have him a credit for righteousness. It can be the same for us! We have scriptures that help us to believe God. *"I am watching over My word to perform it"* (Jeremiah 1:12). *"For I the LORD will speak, and whatever word I speak will be performed"* (Ezekiel 12:25).

When we choose to believe the promises of God, negative thoughts are omitted because God makes our minds alive again. Every scripture in the Bible is a promise from God and all we need to hold onto is one of them.

Abraham Kept Believing God and Moved Forward

Abraham got weary. He lived through a season of uncertainty and negative thinking. In conjunction with what God promised Abraham, the Prophet Isaiah encourages us that if we keep believing God through weariness, then He will strengthen us and cause us to move forward.

> *"Have you never heard? Have you never understood? The LORD is the everlasting God, the Creator of all the earth. He never grows weak or weary. No one can measure the depths of his understanding.*
>
> *He gives power to the weak and strength to the powerless. Even youths will become weak and tired and young men will fall in exhaustion. But those who trust in the LORD will find new strength. They will*

soar high on wings like eagles. They will run and not grow weary. They will walk and not faint." (Isaiah 40:28-31)

This passage gives a divine demonstration of the faith factor, where faith collaborates with action. Although Abraham grew weary, he continued to believe God and move forward. Faith and action became allies in his thinking processes until he received the promise. The faith factor contributed to the fulfillment of God's promise to make Abraham great. Just as God fulfilled His promises to Abraham, He will also make us great because He is no respecter of persons (Romans 2:11; Galatians 3:28).

Emotions and disappointments can cloud our thinking, trials can sap our strength, and temptation can cause us to question and doubt God's promises. In these challenging times, we should seek God for a fresh experience with Him so we have a deep sense of His presence and reassurance from His Word! This will cause us to continue to move forward, believing God and by the faith factor, He will count it as righteousness.

Principles and Precepts for Transforming Our Thinking

"And do not be conformed to this world [any longer with its superficial values and customs], but be transformed and progressively changed [as you mature spiritually] by the renewing of your mind [focusing on godly values and ethical attitudes], so that you may prove [for yourselves] what the will of God is, that which is good and acceptable and perfect [in His plan and purpose for you]" (Romans 12:2, AMP).

Principle-a universal law that is true in any context, situation, or environment.

Precept-life lessons indicating the way one should act or behave.

Practice-the act of rehearsing a behavior over and over, for the purpose of improving or mastering it.

Chapter 4 Reflection Practices

1. What have you learned about yourself from this chapter? Do you ever have an attitude of indifference? Do you consider this attitude to be negative? How can you convert the attitude of indifference to an attitude of gratitude?

2. The faith factor is a collaboration of faith and action. Consider a time where you had faith that was not coupled with action. Select two to three principles and precepts from this chapter and incorporate them into a plan to move forward.

3. When Abraham became weary from the wait of God's promise, God appeared to him in a vision and used the stars to gave him a visual display of the number of his seed. During your devotion time, ask God to show you affirmation of one of His promises to you.

4. Reflect upon the content of this chapter. What strategies can be used to overcome negative thinking using your *F.A.I.T.H.* (Forward Action In Trusting Him) and *A.C.T.I.O.N.* (Activated Confidence, Triumphant In Overcoming Negativity)?

Chapter 5

GUARDING THE GATE OF WHAT WE THINK

"Be very careful about what you think. Your thoughts run your life" (Proverbs 4:23, ICB)

Guarding the Gate of the Heart

Proverbs 23:7a states, *"As a man thinks in his heart, so is he."* Think means "to act as a gatekeeper" in the original Hebrew. A gate is an entry way designed to let things in or keeps things out. Our eyes and ears act as gates or entry ways to our entire body.

What the eyes see, and the ears hear affect our thinking and then impact our entire being. Some people believe that the primary entryway to our soul (mind, emotions, and will) is through the eye-gate and the ear-gate. It is important that we guard these gates because they impact us significantly. We have the power of choice and we must determine to make better choices of what we allow to enter by the eye-gate and the ear-gate. Further, making choices that bless you and not burden you is critical in overcoming negative thinking.

> *What we see and hear affects our thinking and impacts our entire being.*

God is serious about us diligently guarding our hearts. The New Living translation of Proverbs 4:23 reads, *"Guard your heart above all else, for it determines the course of your life."* The phrase "guarding your heart" paints a picture of a sentry or watchman who is keenly focused upon his charge, acutely aware of every movement around him. As the heart pumps blood into all parts of the body, the heart supplies life to the entire being of a person. The heart is roughly the size of a fist and sits in the middle of our chest, slightly to the left. It is the muscle at the center of our circulation system, pumping blood around our bodies as our hearts beat. This blood sends oxygen and nutrients to all parts of your body and carries away unwanted carbon dioxide and waste products. Every extremity of the body is kept alive by the work of the heart.[41] If your natural heart stops functioning, then you stop functioning!

Stay in love with God. Solomon provides the same importance to protecting the heart spiritually, *"Keep thy heart with all diligence; for out of it are the issues of life"* (Proverbs 4:23, KJV). In the original Hebrew, issues carry the meaning of "a

---

[41] https://www.livescience.com/34655-human-heart.html. Accessed January 18, 2020.

territory or its border, the place where one departs a given territory; to bring out or come out."[42] Issues may also refer to "a movement away from a specific point or place."[43] Jude 21 admonishes us to *"keep yourselves in the love of God, looking for the mercy of our Lord Jesus Christ unto eternal life."* Here, the word keep speaks of a prison term or a term of incarceration. God wants us to lock ourselves in His love! Jesus is the base and the boundary, the beauty and the balance, the sum and the substance of all that we are or ever hope to be, but it is our responsibility to keep ourselves in God's love.

Therefore, we can conclude that Jude is telling us not to move away from the boundary or territory of God's love! We cannot allow life's issues to cause us to move away from the love of God.

> *We have the power to control our thoughts by controlling what enters our ear and eye gates when we guard our hearts (Proverbs 4:23).*

Think about how Joseph stayed in love with God during temptation. *"One day, though, he went into the house to do his work. None of the household servants were inside. Potiphar's wife grabbed Joseph by his outer garment and demanded "Let's have some sex!" Instead, Joseph ran outside, leaving his outer garment*

---

[42] W.E. Vines Expository Dictionary of Old and New Testament Words. Wordsearch Bible Software Version 12, 2012. Accessed January 18, 2020.
[43] IBID. Accessed January 18, 2020.

still in her hand" (Genesis 39:11-12, ISV). Joseph controlled his thinking, the images he visualized, and the actions he took.

Instead of being lured into sin based on what he heard (*ear-gate*) and saw (*eye-gate*), he ran (*acted*). Joseph stayed in love with God because he refused to sin against God (Genesis 39:8-9). By guarding what entered his eye and ear gates, Joseph guarded the gate of his heart. He refused to let outside factors keep his heart from being incarcerated and surrounded by God's love.

Do not become bitter. After being sold into slavery by his brothers, and imprisoned because of the lie of Potiphar's wife, Joseph was brought before Pharaoh to interpret his dream and subsequently became second in command (Genesis 41:17-40). During his waiting period, Joseph did not allow his heart to become bitter. He guarded the gate of his heart and it made him better.

Guarding the Heart Against Distractions

In this era of technology, distractions can be both ever-present and enticing. Emails, instant messaging, googling, ecommerce, iTunes are all potential distractions on our smartphones and computers. Distractions come in many forms because there is always something to buy, a video to listen to, a petition to sign and forward, or an interesting post.

Focusing on what's important becomes even more challenging because distractions take your attention from what you are supposed to be doing. Distractions can come from without or within. Internal distractions may be the result of our own internal drives. This can include our thoughts, our conflicts, or our emotions. External distractions result from something outside of yourself. Resist the temptation to answer every "ding" or "swoosh" by scheduling a specific time for email, instant messaging, and text messaging.

You will increase your productivity by maintaining your focus on the task before you. There are all types of distractions that confront us daily. What we want to highlight in this portion of the book is that it is essential that we are aware of the possibility of distractions and that we decide whether to address or ignore the distractions when they occur. Decide if what has just invaded your time and focus is worth your attention. If not, ignore it. If it is worth your attention, attend to it later! Keep your focus on your immediate purpose. We see distraction occur in Mary and Martha's encounter with Jesus as He entered their village. Let's briefly review their story:

> *"As they continued their travel, Jesus entered a village. A woman by the name of Martha welcomed him and made him feel quite at home. She had a sister, Mary, who sat before the Master, hanging on every word he said. But Martha was pulled away by all she had to do in the kitchen. Later, she stepped in, interrupting them.*
>
> *Master, don't you care that my sister has abandoned the kitchen to me? Tell her to lend me a hand." The Master said, "Martha, dear Martha, you're fussing far too much and getting yourself worked up over nothing. One thing only is essential, and Mary has chosen it—it's the main course and won't be taken from her." (Luke 10:38-42, MSG)*

The English Standard Version of Luke 10:40 says that Martha was distracted, which means "to be overly occupied about a thing or to be drawn away" in the original Greek. The passage outlines three distractions that are important to guard our hearts against. Martha was distracted by busyness, a loss of God's perspective, and missing what was essential.

Busyness

Busyness doesn't have to result in stress, but it often does. *Stress* can turn into some ugly situations.

When you have to squeeze in lunch with your spouse or children, you may be too busy and may need to rethink your priorities. Jesus' ministry calendar was *definitely busy,* but He never lost sight of His priorities or focus to seek and to save the lost (Luke 19:10). Busyness can affect our relationships, the quality of our time with others, the depth of our faith, the extent to which we take care of our health, and our willingness and ability to serve others.

Luke tells us the story of how Martha loved others and ministered to them sometimes using her own home as a center for caring. However, Martha had a problem. She was distracted by her kitchen duties and became irritated and critical of her sister Mary (Luke 10:40). Martha apparently had substantial financial means because she had the ability to entertain Jesus and His large group. She was a highly active lady who took initiative and seemed to manage things well. She also looked after her brother and sister who lived with her.

Her focus was on the things of this world—food, necessities, cares, and social entertaining—that had distracted her. Martha became so tired and fatigued, so pressured and tense by busyness that she lost sight of God's perspective.

A Loss of God's Perspective

Perspective is how we perceive people, situations, ideas, or ideals. It is informed by our personal experience, which makes it as unique as anything could be. Our perspective shapes our life by affecting our choices. When we lose perspective, our ability to operate spiritually and rationally goes out the window. Everything we've accomplished in life, the lessons we've learned, the hard times we've overcome, and the ways in which we've grown are discounted when perspective is lost. The driver who is consumed with road rage and pulls into the turning lane just to go around us has lost perspective. Everyone else is stuck in the same traffic.

Doing something dangerous is only going to save him a few seconds in travel time. A loss of perspective makes us say and do things we may regret when our minds become blinded. Satan is the god of this world and he blinds minds by causing people to focus upon self instead of God (2 Corinthians 4:4). How does this apply to Martha? She interrupts Jesus and inquires, *"Lord, don't you care that my sister has left me to do the work by myself? Tell her to help me!"* (Luke 10:40, NIV). Our perspective is the way we see or think about something. Martha's perspective was that Jesus didn't care and that Mary was neglectful in helping her.

Helen Keller, a blind philanthropist and an adviser to four United States presidents once said, *"The greatest tragedy in the world is to have sight and not be able to see."*[44] Miss Keller's perspective of sight is almost an indictment for us as the people of God that lose our perspective.

Martha lost God's perspective because she allowed herself to be distracted as anyone of us can become when we do not guard our hearts from distractions. Yet, Jesus lovingly says, *"Martha, dear Martha, you're fussing far too much and getting yourself worked up over nothing. One thing only is essential, and Mary has chosen it—it's the main course and won't be taken from her"* (Luke 10: 41-42, MSG). Because Martha lost perspective, she missed what was really essential.

Missing the Essential

Essential denotes that which is "vitally important, necessary and indispensable; the basic part or nature of something."[45] Jesus gives Martha a refresher course on His perspective. Martha missed the essential while her sister, Mary, sat at Jesus' feet and took in every work that He spoke (Luke 10: 39). Mary did not lose perspective, so she did not miss the essential!

In contrast, Martha was focused on cleaning the house, washing the dishes, selecting the proper the table settings and decorations, preparing the meal for all of the guests, serving the meal, and cleaning afterwards. Mary sat down at Jesus feet and was hanging on every word that He spoke because she understood that His words were essential! Mary let nothing

---

[44] https://www.brainyquote.com/quotes/helen_keller_383771. Accessed January 18, 2020.

[45] https://www.macmillandictionary.com/us/dictionary/american/essential. Accessed January 18, 2020.

distract her from her *devotion with* the Lord. No matter *how* important anything else is, sitting at Jesus' feet is the one essential thing that is to be given priority. Martha sought to please Jesus with her service and ministering, but she was trying to do too much!

> *If we lose perspective, we will certainly miss what is essential!*

There is always a balance to life and ministry, but the priority is to sit at the feet of Jesus where the main course is served.

Martha was not thinking about the essential because her focus was on the activity of ministry. And ministry is important, but what we may think is important may not be the *most* important. Jesus helps his mother, Mary, to understand this truth.

In Luke 2:49, Jesus says to His mother, *"How is it that ye sought me? Did you not understand that I must be about my Father's business?"* When our daily work, our tasks, and assignments are focused on the Father's business, He will direct us to what is most important and keep us from being distracted by activity that does not always equate to effective ministry. There is always a balance to life and ministry! Missing the essential can also apply to family, friends, and your calling. Sometimes, it's easy to forget just how much family means. Family is irreplaceable and precious, so we must devote time and energy to nurturing these invaluable relationships. Every family has dysfunction, but love is always the answer.

People can struggle when they lack authentic friendship. John 15:13 records Jesus as saying, *"Greater love hath no man than this, that a man lay down his life for his friends."* Here, Jesus uses the word *philos*, which denotes sacrificial aspects of friendship that include loyalty, value, and affection.[46] Do you have a network of friends that you can always count on, who are confidantes, who offer support, and hold you accountable? A good friend can sometimes be the voice of God to help you keep perspective. Missing the essential may also include missing your calling or determining and pursuing your sense of *purpose*. Your calling gives your life purpose and fills you with a sense of energy and vitality that makes everything easier. Your calling is your life's work. It's your legacy.

> *"There is no passion to be found in playing small—in settling for a life that is less than the one you are capable of living."*[47] Nelson Mandela

We can do a lot of things in life and ministry but are they the essential things? Martha, like all of us, needed some help and the help that she needed was to employ the character of God as a gate guard to what she was thinking.

---

[46] W.E. Vines Expository Dictionary of Old and New Testament Words. Wordsearch Bible Software Version 12, 2012. Accessed January 18, 2020.

[47] https://authorsbillboard.com/2018/05/there-is-no-passion-to-be-found-in-playing-small-in-settling-for-a-life-that-is-less-than-the-one-you-are-capable-of-living-nelson-mandela/. Accessed January 18, 2020.

Character: The Gate Guard of What We Think

The primary responsibility of a gate guard is to provide security to an enclosed area such as a corporate building, warehouse, or community. The guard's responsibilities may also include ensuring that unauthorized people or products do not enter or leave the premises or even doing basic maintenance in and around the guarded area. Character is a gate guard to our thinking. There is an acronym to assist with remembering how character has a duty to help us. We must **W.A.T.C.H.**

- **W**-ords
- **A**-ctions
- **T**-houghts
- **C**-ompanions
- **H**-abits

Watch your words. Words have a lot of power, so it's important to be aware of what you are saying. According to the New Living translation, *"the power of the tongue is life and death— those who love to talk will eat what it produces"* (Proverbs 18:21). Our words lead to thoughts, that lead to emotions, which lead to behaviors and beliefs about ourselves. Words frame your world!

Watch your actions. It does not matter who you are, your character will always be defined by your actions. God requires us to act!

Action is required by believers to witness signs, wonders, and miracles (Mark 16:17). Jesus led by example and He was always in action. *"God anointed Jesus of Nazareth with the Holy*

Spirit and with power, and because God was with him, he went around doing good and healing everyone who was oppressed by the devil" (Acts 10:38, IST). We are also called and anointed to *go* around doing good and healing everyone who is oppressed by the devil! If we are going to do good, we must go! (Matthew 28:19-20).

Watch your thoughts. Our thoughts will subsequently produce our words. Our words can create intimacy or separation from God. With our words we can motivate ourselves to do things we never thought we could do and our words can also move others to step forward into their own personal power so they can be of service to their community. Words can calm us or excite us. Words can actually change the direction of a nation. Therefore, watch what you think and be aware of the words that come from your thoughts.

Watch your companions. *"Two are better than one because they have a good reward for their labor; for if they fall, the one will lift up his companion. But woe to the one who falls and does not have another to lift him up!"* (Ecclesiastes 4: 9 – 10). The people with whom we share life are much more important than the things we possess in life. Jointly, two people can work and gain more together. They could produce more and ultimately earn more than they would individually, and they undergird one another. One of my favorite scriptures is Isaiah 43:4: "Since *thou wast precious in my sight, thou hast been honorable, and I have loved thee: therefore will I give men for thee, and people for thy life."* Good companionship will help you. On the other side, 1 Corinthians 15:33 warns us that *"evil companionships corrupt good morals."* Our friends or associates may not be evil, but if they're not actively pursuing the Lord, they can negatively influence us. Their beliefs, ideas, morals, speech, and behavior have the potential to pollute our thinking, weaken us, and ultimately lead us to disobey the Lord.

Watch your habits. If our habits are healthy, our character will be reinforced, and we will be able to adapt and overcome. If our habits are unhealthy, our character will be weakened, and we are unable to adapt to the many unexpected changes in life. The Bible provides principles and precepts that we are to practice regularly to form habits. For instance, Titus 2:7 advises, *"In all things showing yourself to be a pattern of good works; in doctrine showing integrity, reverence, incorruptibility."* Also, Matthew 6:5 NIV instructs us, *"And when you pray, do not be like the hypocrites, for they love to pray standing in the synagogues and on the street corners to be seen by men. I tell you the truth, they have received their reward in full."* When we practice a truth habitually, we become an example of the truth. Jesus said, *"Keep watch and pray, so that you will not give in to temptation. For the spirit is willing, but the body is weak!"* (Matthew 26:41, NIV).

To keep watch and pray must be a habit of our character. The word watch means "to have the alertness of a guard at night."[48] A night watchman must be even more vigilant than a daytime guard. In the daytime, danger can often be spotted from a distance, but this is not the case at night. A night watchman must use senses other than sight to detect danger. They must be hyper-vigilant, suspecting an assault or attack at any moment because there is usually little or no indication of enemy attack until it happens. This is the type of watching Jesus spoke of in Matthew 26. Our character's duty is to perform in accordance with Jesus' description of the night watchman. Our character is always on duty as the gate guard

---

[48] W.E. Vines Expository Dictionary of Old and New Testament Words. Wordsearch Bible Software Version 12, 2012. Accessed January 18, 2020.

of what we think. When we practically apply the principles and precepts of **WATCH,** our character becomes a guard and a guide for what we think.

Do We Really Know What Character Is?

We have used the word character throughout this chapter and people use it frequently, but do we really know what character means? Character is the stuff that makes something what it is. If you're currently sitting in a chair while reading this book, the character of your chair may include wood, metal, a foam cushion, screws and perhaps plastic. The stuff that makes the chair a chair. When a person is said to have good character, it all comes down to a person's core values and to their motivations for acting as they do. In general, people who are considered to have good character often have traits like integrity, honesty, courage, loyalty, fortitude, and other important virtues that promote good, moral behavior. These character traits define who they are as people and highly influence the choices they make. The following are a few thoughts concerning the nature of character.

> *"Be careful of your thoughts, for your thoughts become your words. Be careful of your words, for your words become your deeds. Be careful of your deeds, for your deeds become your habits. Be careful of your habits, for your habits become your character. Be careful of your character, for your character becomes your destiny."* – Chinese Proverb

"Watch your thoughts. They become words. Watch your words. They become deeds. Watch your deeds. They become habits. Watch your habits. They become character. Character is everything." – Ralph Waldo Emerson

"Character shapes the destiny of an individual person. In fact, character shapes the destiny of an entire society, for within the character of the citizen lies the welfare of the nation." – Cicero

The preceding thoughts on character provide us with a valuable compass for navigating life and ministry. Yet, no discussion of character is complete without a discussion of the nature of biblical character.

The Substance of Biblical Character

Biblical principles shape our Christian faith and give us life. What does the Bible say about character? I believe Hebrews 1:3 provides an answer. The New Living Translation reads: *"The Son radiates God's own glory and expresses the very character of God, and he sustains everything by the mighty power of his command."* The King James Version says, *"Who being the brightness of his glory, and the express image of His person, and upholding all things by the word of his power..."* Here, express image speaks of character. It means the very stamp, mark, and impression, the reproduction of God. The writer utilizes the imagery and connotation of a king or governor and his signet ring.

In that era, a ruler would place his signet ring in hot wax to authenticate a document with his seal before sending it throughout his territory. The ruler's image was official, and it was as if the emperor or governor himself was present in representing his word.[49] The image became the substance or the character of the ruler's word. Similarly, the word of the Lord is the character, the substance, the impression, and the mark of God's authority in the earth.

> *The Word of God is the character, substance, impression, and mark of His authority in the earth.*

According to W.E. Vines Expository Dictionary of Old and New Testament Words, image is translated in this passage as *eikon,* which means representation and manifestation.

The image of Christ is exhibited as a representation and manifestation of God. This is the impression (character) in representation (image) that is the brightness of God's glory described above in Hebrews 1:3a. Jesus Christ is the impression and image of God personified. He is the reproduction of God's character and nature. He is that which makes Him who He is and who we are to become. In other words, a person could look at Jesus Christ and see exactly what God is like because of His character is rooted in love.

---

[49] Preacher's Outline and Sermon Bible Commentary. Wordsearch Bible Software Version 12, 2012. Accessed January 18, 2020.

The substance of biblical character is further expressed in Galatians 5:22-25 as the fruit of the Spirit. The Amplified Version reads:

> *"But the fruit of the Spirit [the result of His presence within us] is love [unselfish concern for others], joy, [inner] peace, patience [not the ability to wait, but how we act while waiting], kindness, goodness, faithfulness, gentleness, self-control. Against such things, there is no law. And those who belong to Christ Jesus have crucified the sinful nature together with its passions and appetites. If we [claim to] live by the [Holy] Spirit, we must also walk by the Spirit [with personal integrity, Godly character, and moral courage — our conduct empowered by the Holy Spirit]."*

Fruit is the natural product of a living thing. Paul used the word fruit to help us understand the character, the nature of what is produced within the believer by the Holy Spirit who lives within. The fruit of the Spirit is the character of God produced by the Spirit, not by the Christian. As we grow and mature, all the characteristics of Christ seen and experienced in the fruit of the Spirit will be manifested in our lives!

Next, we will discuss 1 Samuel 14: 6-7 to outline a model that Jonathan's armor-bearer provides on biblical character. From the Amplified Version:

> *"Jonathan said to his young armor-bearer, "Come, let us cross over to the garrison of these uncircumcised men; it may be that the LORD will work for us. For there is nothing to prevent the LORD from saving,*

> *whether by many or by few." And his armor-bearer*
> *said to him, "Do everything that is in your heart*
> ***(mind); here I am with you in whatever* you think**
> *is best."*

The Philistines had mobilized a huge army with thousands of chariots and division after division of foot soldiers. They were poised to attack and prepared to subject the Israelites to oppression. Raiding parties had been sent out by the Philistines to harass, plunder, and demoralize the Israelite population. In one of the most daring and fearless feats by an individual in military history, Jonathan and his armor-bearer climbed the face of a dangerous, jagged cliff that was actually flanked by two rock formations. In the face of this danger, Jonathan believed that the Lord could and would save His people. His armor-bearer's response revealed the substance of his character. I believe the substance of Jonathan's character (faith in God) stirred the substance of his armor-bearer' character (loyalty to Jonathan in heart and mind). In the original Hebrew, the word heart is translated as *leb*, which is "the seat of emotion." Leb is sometimes translated "to think" and it is the place where commitments are determined, kept, or broken.[50]

Character determines the course of your life! How does this relate to guarding the gate of what we think? Recall that character guards the gate to what we think. Although Jonathan and his armor-bearer were confronted with a significant emotional event, their character (the gate guard to their thinking) was in place and functioning.

---

[50] W.E. Vines Expository Dictionary of Old and New Testament Words. Wordsearch Bible Software Version 12, 2012. Accessed January 18, 2020.

They succeeded where others most likely would have failed! Their character functioned with steadfast confidence and faith in God. They were thinking like God thinks! In conclusion, character is what really determines the course of our life. We cannot lose with the stuff that we use (faith in God) with character as the gate guard of what we think!

Principles and Precepts For Transforming Our Thinking

"And do not be conformed to this world [any longer with its superficial values and customs], but be transformed and progressively changed [as you mature spiritually] by the renewing of your mind [focusing on godly values and ethical attitudes] So that you may prove [for yourselves] what the will of God is, that which is good and acceptable and perfect [in His plan and purpose for you]" (Romans 12:2, AMP).

Principle-a universal law that is true in any context, situation, or environment.

Precept-life lessons indicating the way one should act or behave.

Practice-the act of rehearsing a behavior over and over, for the purpose of improving or mastering it.

Chapter 5 Reflection Practices

1. In guarding the gate of your heart, you must guard your ear and eye gates. Assess your daily activities. Is

there negativity entering your ear and eye gates that have reached your heart? Is it affecting your thinking? What daily practical steps can you take to guard the gate of your heart?

2. Sometimes life brings hard or traumatic experiences that can leave us bitter. When we think like God thinks, we convert these experiences so that they make us better. Consider the life of Joseph. How can you use his life as a model to become better instead of bitter?

3. Read the story of Mary and Martha in Luke 10. Martha was distracted by busyness, a loss of perspective, and missing what was essential. Make a plan that omits these types of distractions and allows time for what is essential (devotion to God, family, friends, your calling, etc.). Then, implement the plan with an accountability partner.

4. From the principles and precepts from this chapter, how can you keep yourself in the love of God (Jude 21) when you must function in a consistently negative environment?

Chapter 6

BEING RENEWED IN THE SPIRIT OF THE MIND

"And be renewed in the spirit of your mind."

Ephesians 4:23

To be renewed means to be made new, readjusted, changed, turned around, and regenerated. It is a process to spiritual renewal. In Ephesians 4:23, Paul is saying to the church that the mind of man has been infected by sin and needs to be made new. Paul reminds the church that the mind is far from perfect. Without the mind of Christ (1 Corinthians 2:16), the mind of man is worldly, selfish, self-centered, and self-seeking. When we don't have the mind of Christ, the mind is blinded and dull with an inability to choose between right and wrong. *"The god of this age has blinded the minds of unbelievers, so that they cannot see the light of the gospel that displays the glory of Christ, who is the image of God"* (2 Corinthians 4:4, NIV).

To assist with understanding how to renew the mind, there are three main components that will be discussed in this chapter:

1. The Futility (Vanity) of the Mind
2. God Holds Our Hand When We Cannot See
3. The Key to Renewing the Mind Is to Choose Life

The Futility (Vanity) of The Mind

I think the first step to renewing the mind is to realize that without God, the mind is blinded. Paul describes a blinded mind when he speaks to the church at Ephesus in the following passage.

> *"So this I say and solemnly testify in [the name of] the Lord [as in His presence], that you must no longer live as the heathen (the Gentiles) do in their perverseness, in the folly, vanity, and emptiness of their souls and the futility of their minds. Their moral understanding is darkened, and their reasoning is beclouded. They are alienated (estranged, self-banished) from the life of God [with no share in it; this is] because of the ignorance (the want of knowledge and perception, the willful blindness) that is deep-seated in them, due to their hardness of heart [to the insensitiveness of their moral nature]."*

(Ephesians 4:17-18, AMP)

Paul stated that the Gentiles lived in the futility of their minds. Futility is the state of "having no effect or of achieving nothing; having little or no purpose or importance." He describes the pointlessness or futility of a person's thought process (their mind) when they have been willfully blinded.

Their hearts become hardened (which lends to a lack of character). Willful blindness is a person's choice, a choice that is made from the soul (mind, emotions, and will) that leads to the pathway of vanity.

> *"Vanity of vanities says the Preacher; all is vanity"* (*Ecclesiastes 12:8, RSV). Vanity influences our thinking and ultimately leaves us empty, void and dissatisfied.*

Hundreds of years prior to Paul's letters to the Corinthians and Ephesians, King Solomon spoke of vanity. He says, *"vanity of vanities, saith the Preacher, vanity of vanities; all is vanity"* (Ecclesiastes 1:2). The Amplified Version interprets the verse as *"vapor of vapors and futility of futilities, says the Preacher. Vapor of vapors and futility of futilities! All is vanity (emptiness, falsity, and vainglory)."* Vanity literally means vapor, breath, or wind. It describes something that is without any value or substance. The word vanity is used 38 times in Ecclesiastes to refer to something that is fleeting and quickly passing away.

Though vanity has an effect and it is felt, its effect does not last but leaves behind an emptiness, a void. As Solomon examined human life, he deduced through experience and experimentation that all things were vain, meaningless, empty because they brought no abiding satisfaction. Whatever effect they might have had lasted only for a fleeting moment.

Solomon concludes the book of Ecclesiastes with an admonishment to *"Remember your Creator"* (Ecclesiastes 12:1). That is, the conclusion is that we must be aware of God and intentionally think about Him again and again. Further, Solomon instructs us to pay attention to God, to consider Him with the intention and determination of obeying. He admonishes us to keep our minds on God. We must allow Him to influence us so that we think like God thinks, to guide us, and to govern our decisions and conduct.

"Now all has been heard; here is the conclusion of the matter: Fear God and keep his commandments, for this is the whole [duty] of man" (Ecclesiastes 12:13-14, NIV). We must think like God thinks because *"there is a way that seems right to a man, but its end is the way to death"* (Proverbs 14:12). Adam and Eve died the day that they leaned on their own thoughts and failed to think of God. They were separated from God based on what they thought of God (Genesis 3:3, 24).

Their thoughts became vain imaginations. Humanity has been infected with this syndrome from that day to this day. Without Christ, no matter what our occupational, educational, or economic achievements may be, we are still in the dark, blinded to the truth. The solution is God and He will help us to overcome vanity. We will conclude this portion of the chapter with a couple of scriptures regarding vanity with a brief discussion of each.

> *"When they knew God, they glorified him not as God, neither were thankful; but became vain in their imaginations, and their foolish heart was darkened."* (Romans 1:21)

The word "imaginations" means thoughts, reasonings, deliberations, conclusions, and speculations. We should not allow our thoughts to become vain because this will lead to emptiness.

> *"The LORD knows the thoughts of man, that they are vanity."* (Psalm 94:11)

God knows that our thoughts can be meaningless and without value. He instructs us to renew our minds to combat vanity and God will hold our hand through the process.

God Holds Our Hand When We Cannot See

At 7 years old, Helen Keller became physically blind. She once stated, "If the blind put their hands in God's hands, they will find their way more surely than those who see but have not faith or purpose." Despite her physical blindness and associated sufferings, she is also remembered for being an accomplished author and activist for people with disabilities, teaching others to persevere in the face of adversity.[51]

Through a life of adversity and hardship, she learned to let God hold her hand when she could not see. Think about when you were a child and your parents took you by the hand as you were crossing the street or in a crowded mall. It was a measure of safety and security for your parents, knowing that the well-being of their child was in their hands. You may recall that you did not want your parents to hold your hands on some occasions! However, your parents knew that you did

---

[51] https://www.hki.org/helen-kellers-life-and-legacy. Accessed November 26, 2019.

not have the experience in life as a child that they possessed as parents. So, they held your hand anyway because they loved you and knew you were theirs. God treats us the same way!

David talks about God holding his hand when he could not see. *"You've given me the shield of your salvation; your strong hand has supported me; your help has made me great"* (Psalm 18:35, CEB). As David reflected on his battles, he testified that God had equipped him with everything he needed to be victorious. God had led and strengthened him every step of the way, through dangers seen and unseen.

David further says to the Lord, *"My soul clings to you; your right hand upholds me"* (Psalm 63:8). Like David, God wants us to confess our dependence on Him so that He can strengthen and uphold us in His hand, guiding us through every crisis and conflict. When we renew our minds, we resolve that God is right, He sees what we cannot see, and that His strength is greater than ours.

The Key to Renewing the Mind Is To Choose Life

You may be familiar with Deuteronomy Chapter 28, where Moses instructs the Israelites on the rewards for following God and the consequences if they did not. Take a moment to read the chapter. In verses 1–14, the predominant themes are prosperity, success, and God's favor if they obey God. In the English Standard Version of Deuteronomy chapter 28, the word *blessings* is used ten times within verses 1– 14. Moses also speaks of abounding in prosperity, increase, defeating their enemies, opening His good treasury, and blessing the work of their hands.

In contrast, for verses 15-68, God very clearly speaks of Israel's destruction for failing to obey His commands. He tells His people eight times that they will be *cursed* if they do not obey. To be cursed speaks of being "injured; subjected to evil; to be vexed, harassed or tormented with great calamities, to be devoted to destruction." Moreover, God's penalty for disobedience is listed as confusion, frustration, destruction, becoming perished, victims of plagues and pestilence, defeat before enemies, becoming a horror to others, madness and blindness, poverty, oppression, victims of robbery, enslavement to others, forced to serve other gods, and lack of help.

Choose life. Obedience brought the Israelites blessings (life) and disobedience resulted in cursing's (death). Moses lets the people know that it was their decision as to what they received.

> *"Today I have given you the choice between life and death, between blessings and curses. Now I call on heaven and earth to witness the choice you make. Oh, that you would choose life, so that you and your descendants might live! You can make this choice by loving the Lord your God, obeying him, and committing yourself firmly to him. This is the key to your life."* (Deuteronomy 30:19, NLT)

Moses gave two strong reasons why the people must choose life, why they must live a life dedicated to God where they renewed their commitment and covenant with Him. To renew their commitment and covenant, they had to first renew their minds to their commitment and covenant! Their minds were not renewed because the commandments, statutes, and ordinances in God's covenant had come to seem like nothing but a burden to Israel. When we renew our minds and allow our minds to be saturated with the revelation that the Lord is my life, then the choice is easy to make the commitment and choose life!

> *To renew a commitment or covenant, we must first renew our mind to the commitment or covenant.*

When God told Moses to tell His people to choose life in Deuteronomy 30:19, it is the same life that Jesus called the abundant life in John 10:10. This life is derived from *zoe*, which means "to live." This type of life is the energy, the catalyst, the force, and the power of being. The life that God gives does not include perishing; it is eternal. It is deliverance from condemnation and death. It is the cessation of deterioration, decay, and corruption (John 3:16; John 5:24, 29; John 10:28). It is the very life of God Himself!

The life that God gives does not just refer to duration, but it references the donation of our lives in the earth. When we choose God, our lives can consistently know love, joy, peace, power, and responsibility in the earth before we get to heaven. It is a life of satisfaction because He is the Satisfier! It has been unveiled and is clearly seen that Jesus Christ shows man what life is (John 1:4-5; John 5:26; 1 John 1:2) and this life only comes to a man or woman by believing in Jesus Christ.

For the remainder of the chapter, we will discuss other techniques that can be used to renew the mind.

Allow the Spirit to Renew Your Mind

A man or woman outside of Jesus Christ only exists. Existing is not necessarily living. Most people need an epiphany to unveil this truth. *"And ye shall know the truth, and the truth shall make you free"* (Romans 8:32). We frequently exist in a world of negativity. Therefore, we must renew our minds daily to set us free from the world's gravity of negativity. In fact, this is the only way to overcome negative thinking. The Spirit of the Lord is the source to renew our minds. Allow the Spirit of the Lord to speak to you and renew your mind as you read over these scriptures:

> *"The Spirit of the Lord is upon me, because he hath anointed me to preach the gospel to the poor; he hath sent me to heal the brokenhearted, to preach deliverance to the captives and recovering of sight to the blind. To set at liberty them that are bruised. To preach the acceptable year of the Lord."* (Luke 4:18-19)

Our minds are renewed when we lean and depend on the source of our power, which is the Spirit of the Lord.

> *"When the Spirit of truth comes, he will guide you into all the truth, for he will not speak on his own authority, But whatever he hears he will speak, and*

> *he will declare to you the things that are to come."*
> (John 16:13, ESV)

Our minds are renewed when know that the Spirit of the Lord guides us to truth and tells us things to come. The Holy Spirit speaks only the truth and guides us into all truth. The renewing of our minds begins with the Spirit of the Lord.

Realize that You Have Power Over the Enemy

The Amplified version of Luke 10:19 states, *"God has given us authority and power to trample upon serpents and scorpions, and [physical and mental strength and ability] over all the power that the enemy [possesses]; and nothing shall in any way harm you."* Our minds are renewed when we realize that God has given us the ability in our minds (mental strength) to reject and resist the power of the enemy! So, we must solidify in our hearts (character) that we have more power and ability than the devil.

Jesus boldly declares this truth in John 14:30, *"The ruler of this world is coming, but he has no power over me* (CEV). The ruler of this world (Satan) will never stop coming. He will always attempt to come with lies, deceptions, depression, frustration, disappointment, irritation, fear, anxiety, and discouragement. These negative thoughts and emotions are all a part of his warfare strategies.

As we consistently and constantly tap into our power source to renew our minds, the enemy's strategies lose the ability to distract or hinder us in life and ministry. The latter portion of Isaiah 59:19 reminds us, *"When the enemy shall come in like a flood, the Spirit of the Lord shall lift up a standard against him."* I especially like the New Living translation: *"When the enemy comes like a raging flood tide, the Spirit of the Lord will drive him back!"* When I reflect and digest this truth, my mind is renewed because I know that the ruler of this world has no power over me!

Rehearse the Word

The renewing of our mind is the constant practice of rehearsing God's Word. To rehearse is to "re-hear." Each time we re-hear His Word, it gives us life and renews our minds. God is our life because *"in Him we live and move and have our being"* (Acts 17:28). Psalm 119:105 reminds us that, *"God's Word is a lamp unto my feet, and a light unto my path."* It is the lamp of God's Word that directs our steps.

The light of God's word shows us the path to take to a renewed mind.

Acknowledge that God Is The Key To Your Life

When you renew your mind, you recognize that God is the key to your life (Deuteronomy 30:19). A key grants access, but the same key can also deny access. Positive thinking grants access while negative thinking denies access. Positive thinking is choosing life. Since the Lord is the key to our lives, with positive thinking (thinking His Word) we have access to the Lord's battle plans when we are attacked (Deuteronomy 28:7), abundant prosperity (Deuteronomy 28:11), and a plethora of other benefits outlined in the scriptures.

Know That You Have More than Potential

The fairy tale *"The Little Engine That Could"* holds a powerful precept. A train carrying toys and treats for good children breaks down. Three of the train engines decide not to help for various reasons.

Finally, a little blue engine comes along and helps the little engine. The story's signature phrase "I think I can, I think I can" first occurred in print in a 1902 article in a Swedish journal.[52] The blue engine was thinking like God thinks. The little engine thought that he could, and he did! Renew your mind! Know that you have more than just potential, you can do it!

> *Know that you have more than potential. You can do it!*

Rehearse these truths: "I *can do all things through him who strengthens me*" (Philippians 4:13). *"Arise, for it is your task, and we are with you; be strong and do it"* (Ezra 10:4). *"[You say to Me,] 'If You can?' All things are possible for the one who believes and trusts [in Me]!"* (Mark 9:23, AMP).

Declare Your *Faith* and Not Your *Fears*

It is important that we have the right attitude. One's attitude reflects how one thinks, feels, and behaves in a given

---

[52] Plotnick, Roy E. (2012). "In Search of Watty Piper: The History of the Little Engine Story." New Review of Children's Literature and Librarianship. 18 (1): 11–26

situation. Attitude can also be defined as "our response to people, places, things, or events in life."[53] David was honest and developed the skill at having the right attitude about his struggles and fears.

Take a look at Psalm 27:1. *"The Lord is my light and my salvation; whom shall I fear? The Lord is the strength of my life; of whom shall I be afraid?"* David did not begin this psalm by stating his fears, instead he declared his faith. In so doing, he identified the only solution to the problem of fear, which was trusting the Lord. David testifies that God is his light, salvation, and strength. David's mindset was not to be afraid of anything or anyone because of his personal relationship with the Lord.

Develop Good Thinking Habits

Habits are routine behaviors done on a regular basis and acquired through frequent repetition. Our thought habits affect every aspect of our lives, which subsequently shapes our mindset. Our mindset then impacts how we view or make sense of the world, and how we make sense of self and others.[54]

According to a 2009 study, researchers from University College London examined the new habits of 96 people over the space of 12 weeks. The study discovered that the average time it takes to form or create a new habit is 66 days (not the more familiar 21 days that we are more accustomed to hearing).

---

[53] https://psychologenie.com/types-of-attitudes. Accessed November 26, 2019.

[54] http://sourcesofinsight.com/what-is-mindset/. Accessed November 28, 2019.

Furthermore, the study revealed that individual times varied from 18 days to 254 days depending upon the person.

Here are some important takeaways from the study:

o It may take up to two months to develop a new habit.
o Don't despair if 21 days does not work. For most people that's simply not enough time.[55]
o Practicing positive thinking creates habits that you can depend on in time of crisis.

With the Lord as the key to our lives, we must practice our faith and trust in our Coach. It is God that renews the spirit of our minds. We can do our part by creating good thought habits and recurrent patterns of biblical behaviors through frequent repetition. The thought habits will then cultivate our mindset to one that overcomes negative thoughts by depending on God.

Principles and Precepts For Transforming Our Thinking

"And do not be conformed to this world [any longer with its superficial values and customs], but be transformed and progressively changed [as you mature spiritually] By the renewing of your mind [focusing on godly values and ethical attitudes], so that you may prove [for yourselves] what the will of God is, that which is good and acceptable and perfect [in His plan and purpose for you]" (Romans 12:2, AMP).

---

[55] https://www.sciencealert.com/how-long-it-takes-to-break-a-habit-according-to-science. Accessed November 28, 2019

Principle-a universal law that is true in any context, situation, or environment.

Precept-life lessons indicating the way one should act or behave.

Practice-the act of rehearsing a behavior over and over, for the purpose of improving or mastering it.

Chapter 6 Reflection Practices

1. God is the key to our lives, but we have the power to open or shut doors. Positive thinking is the key to gaining access and negative thinking causes access to be denied. What negative thinking has shut doors in your life? How has positive thinking opened doors?

2. In order to renew a commitment or covenant, you must first renew your mind concerning that commitment or covenant. Have you ever tried to repair a relationship (marriage, friendship, coworker) without changing your thoughts? What was the result?

3. Places where we have negative attitudes, irritation and frustration, or anxiety and fear are usually points where we need to have our minds renewed. Consider such a place for you. Look up scriptures that speak to the situation. Spend 15 - 30 minutes each day rehearsing God's Word concerning the matter. Remember that it could take two or more months to change your mental habits.

Chapter 7

THINK ABOUT ELEVATING YOUR MIND

*"Since you have been raised to new life with Christ,
set your sights on the realities of heaven, where Christ
sits in the place of honor at God's right hand.*

*Think about the things of heaven, not the things of
earth. For you died to this life, and your real life is
hidden with Christ in God."* (Colossians 3:1-3, NLT)

Keep the Main Thing the Main Thing

In his book, *7 Habits of Highly Effective People*, Stephen Covey gives a philosophy that encourages us to keep the main thing the main thing. As it relates to overcoming negative thinking, this precept means creating thought habits that focus on what is important. This is a technique that enables us to elevate our minds. When we think like God thinks, we *"think about the things of heaven, not the things of earth"* (Colossians 3:3, NLT).

This precept is further cultivated for the believer because when we receive Jesus Christ as Lord and Savior, we understand that our life is hidden in Christ, who is the main thing! The King James Version of Colossians 3:2 advises *"Set your affection on things above, not on things on the earth."* The Greek word used for set in this verse means "to seek after, strive for, be intent on" and the term affection represents "the mind."[56]

Paul tells the church at Colosse that this must be the way that they choose to live. It is not a one-time event that happens and is quickly forgotten. It's a way of living that allows us to be set free when we think like God thinks (on the things above) instead of the gravity of negativity in the world (on the things of earth). Elevating our minds is to look at life with the viewpoint that we are hidden with Christ in God so that we view life from God's vantage point.

God Is Our Divine Elevator

Man has a spirit, soul, and body (1 Thessalonians 5:23). The body primarily deals with the five senses, the soul refers to the emotions, and the spirit of man references our God consciousness. According to Proverbs 20:27, *"the spirit of man is the lamp of the Lord, searching all his innermost parts* (ESV). God has instilled an awareness of Him within us so that our spirit knows that He exists. Part of that awareness is a conscience about right and wrong. Therefore, Proverbs 20:27 can be interpreted that our conscience (thinking) is God's light that searches our innermost being and tells us if we are doing

---

[56] Practical Word Studies In The New Testament, Word Search Bible Software, Version 12, 2012, Accessed December 25, 2019.

right or wrong. Our conscience (thinking) is God's light that searches our innermost being and tells us right from wrong.

Take a look at the Amplified Version of Proverbs 20:27, *"The spirit of man [that factor in human personality which proceeds immediately from God] is the lamp of the Lord, searching all his innermost parts."*

The spirit of man, the heart, is the lamp of the Lord. This means that God will lead us by *"His Spirit in our human spirit."* Only when our hearts are right and pure, can we trust what our heart tells us. When our hearts are right and pure, we can clearly hear and truly be led by the Spirit. This process results in elevated thinking. It is important to note that elevating our minds acknowledges our need for direction and guidance from our Divine Elevator (God) every day.

The Bible responds to the reality of this need, speaking of the Lord, *"Your word is a lamp to my feet and a light for my path"* (Psalm 119:105, NIV). The psalmist announced unashamedly that God's Word had been the guide for his life. David knew that God was His Divine Elevator.

> *Making the effort to elevate our minds means that we acknowledge the need for direction and guidance from God, our Divine Elevator.*

Choose the Narrow Gate

"Enter through the narrow gate. For wide is the gate and broad is the road that leads to destruction, and many enter through it. But small is the gate and narrow the road that leads to life, and only a few find it" (Matthew 7:13-14, NIV). There are two gates, one wide and one narrow. The wide gate is the way of the world. It is immediately before us when we are born. The narrow gate, which is the way of salvation, is not seen. Consistently and individually we must search for the narrow gate. God challenges us as His people declaring *"And ye shall seek me, and find me, when ye shall search for me with all your heart"* (Jeremiah 19:13) and *"I'm setting before you the way of life and the way of death"* (Jeremiah 21:8, CEB). As we think about elevating our minds, we must choose the narrow gate each day.

Hate Every Wrong Thought

"How sweet are your words to my taste, sweeter than honey to my mouth! "I gain understanding from your precepts; therefore, I hate every wrong path" (Psalm 119:103-104, NIV).

The writer experienced an elevation of his mind. He learned to love the precepts and principles of God so much that he described them with vivid word pictures. He also learned to hate every wrong path, or every wrong thought. The writer says that he gained understanding from God's precepts, which is evidence of elevated thinking.

How Do You Think About Treasure?

Another essential precept about elevating our minds is contained in Matthew 6:19-21. In this passage Jesus tells His followers:

> *"Do not lay up for yourselves treasures on earth, where moth and rust destroy and where thieves break in and steal, but lay up for yourselves treasures in heaven, where neither moth nor rust destroys and where thieves do not break in and steal. For where your treasure is, there your heart will be also."*

In general, treasures on earth include money and possessions. Now, it is important to know that Jesus did not say that we can't purchase a home, save or invest money for retirement, or have a nice car. Jesus is conveying that he does not want us to focus on accumulating money and possessions and neglect to pursue treasures in heaven. What are heavenly treasures? We are to treasure the Lord Jesus most of all. When Jesus is our treasure, we will commit our resources—our money, our time, and our talents—to His work in this world. Our motivation for our treasures is what is important. Thinking about elevating our minds includes answering questions such as:

o Do I treasure my relationship with Jesus, or do I treasure the things of the world?
o Do I obsess over earning more money or buying more things?
o Am I consumed with living and loving like Jesus?

The answer to these questions will let us know the location of our treasures (earthly or heavenly) and help us to keep the main thing the main thing.

Is Your Devotion Working?

The purpose of a personal devotion to God is individual and personal edification and spiritual formation. There are a multitude of daily devotionals on bookshelves around the globe. We can also access them online and download them to our smartphone or tablet. We have 365-day devotionals, 30-day devotionals, various thematic devotionals, devotionals for men, devotionals for women, devotionals for teens, and devotionals about money. What we have understood as a time of devotion is also a time of prayer to prepare our day. But, is your devotion working? Is your mind being renewed? Is your devotion time elevating your mind daily? I had an experience that left me asking myself these types of questions.

During the coronavirus outbreak of 2020, I had completed my daily devotion and headed to a grocery store to pick up a few items. As I approached the store, there was already a long line of people waiting to enter. It was raining and I exited my car and headed for the awning to get out of the rain. As I stepped under the awning, immediately a man said, "Hey, there is a line!" I swiftly responded, "Is it all right with you if I get out of the rain?" My thoughts begin to race (some of which were negative). Coincidentally (or maybe by the divine hand of God), my devotion theme was "What shall separate us from the love of God?" (Romans 8: 35-39).

As I stood in line, my thoughts went to the character and nature of God. It was a time of learning for me to think like

God thinks. It was sobering for me to think that going to the grocery store to pick up a few items *could* have separated me from showing God's love! As the nation had begun to lock down, people were becoming frantic. I had to think about the guy who thought I was cutting the line.

Had he just lost his job? Was he anxious because there were no diapers for his baby? His response to me really was not about me, it was really about him! Is my devotion to God changing me for the better? How well do I represent the Lord? We must think for a change if we desire to be changed!

> *Change will not come if we wait for some other person or some other time. We are the ones we have been waiting for. We are the change that we seek.*
>
> *Barak Obama*

What Do You Think About Money?

If we are devoted to God and we know that He is our Divine Elevator and we see Jesus as our treasure, then it is vital for many of us to renew our minds about how we think about money. Money affects everything. It affects where we live, what we eat, how we dress, and what we do with our free time. It affects what we can give back to our community. What you spend in one area directly affects how much you have left to spend in the other areas of your life. Money touches all aspects of how we live, how we think, how we feel, and how we dream. Overcoming negative thoughts concerning money will assist us in changing our world.

What do you think about money? The Bible gives us more than 2300 verses on money, wealth and possessions. Jesus spoke about money roughly 15% of his preaching and in 11 out of His 39 parables.

Money was the Lord's most talked about topic! [57] Why is that? I submit that it is because God knows that our attitude toward money is an indication of the state of our heart towards Him. Our perspective of money gets to the heart of the matter. *"For where your treasure is, there your heart will be also"* (Matthew 6:21). Money is important to the extent that how we think about it will impact how we behave with it.

The Bible records King Solomon as the wealthiest man that ever lived. During his 40-year reign, he received approximately $64,300,800,000.[58] Yet, Solomon concluded, *"He who loves money will not be satisfied with money, nor he who loves abundance with its income. This too is vanity"* (Ecclesiastes 5:10, NASB). In Matthew 19:16-24, Jesus tells a rich, young ruler to sell his possessions, give to the poor, and follow Him so that he could get treasures in heaven. The ruler walked away from Jesus in sadness because he had many possessions. The issue wasn't that the young man was rich, but that he treasured his riches above an authentic relationship with Christ. What this really means is that he could not elevate his mind and see Jesus

---

[57] https://wealthwithpurpose.com/god-money/why-does-the-bible-mention-money-so-often/. Accessed December 29, 2019.

[58] https://www.quora.com/What-is-the-estimate-of-king-solomons-wealth-in-todays-economy-and-is-he-the-likely-richest. Accessed December 29, 2019.

as the treasure. If God has given you much, do not allow an ungodly pride to take up residence in your character. Enjoy God's abundance, share it with others in need, and use it for His kingdom and glory!

Be Intentional and Deliberate About Managing Money

Being intentional and deliberate about managing our financial resources must start with tithing. God asks us to give 10% of our resources and a free-will offering to the church where He has planted us (1 Corinthians 12:18). God asks a very pointed question to His people in Malachi 3: 9-11. The Amplified version reads:

> "Will a man rob God? Yet you are robbing Me! But you say, 'In what way have we robbed You?' In tithes and offerings [you have withheld]. You are cursed with a curse, for you are robbing Me, this whole nation! Bring all the tithes (the tenth) into the storehouse, so that there may be food (supplies) in My house, and test Me now in this," says the Lord of hosts, "if I will not open for you the windows of heaven and pour out for you [so great] a blessing until there is no more room to receive it."

The people of Malachi's day needed to elevate their minds concerning the responsibility of the tithe and free-will offering. The tithe was to be a tenth of all the people owned—livestock, harvests, and income from trade or property, or any other source of income (Leviticus 27:30-32). God addressed the mindset of the people because they had no sincere desire to give or to serve the Lord.

They were ungrateful for what the Lord had given them and were unwilling to return anything to Him. The purpose of the tithe was to support the priests and Levites so that the work of the temple could be performed. Tithes and offerings support the work of our modern-day church. The poor and disadvantaged widows, orphans, foreigners, and others in need also benefit from the people's tithes and offerings (Deuteronomy 14:27-29). Without sufficient tithes and offerings, the nation's entire religious system would suffer and, in turn, so would society at large.

Several years ago, while in prayer, I asked God to increase my tithe. To be clear, I was not asking God for more money, I was asking God to increase my tithe for the sake of ministry. I wanted to have the ability to assist others in need. If the Spirit of the Lord spoke to me and said bless a single mother with $1000, then I wanted to have the money available.

This seed was imprinted upon my mind and heart because a physician that I worked for paid for my undergraduate degree and sent my wife and I $500 a month for our expenses! I am grateful and humbled to say that God has increased my tithe and is increasing my tithe because my focus is *not money*. My focus is *ministry*.

As God's people, in representation of Him, we are to be a blessing to others, to be a light and testimony of God's love to the whole world. Tithing is the only principle that God invites us to prove Him on. He promises many blessings if we obey Him in the tithe. When we give our tithe (the first 10%) along with a free will offering, we are really investing in ourselves because God says He will bless us. Tithing and other forms of giving (free will offerings and donations) are intentional, purposeful principles of solid money management. Proverbs 16:3 says, *"Commit to the Lord whatever you do, and your plans will succeed."* Elevate your mind concerning the tithe.

Pray Boldly!

Jabez was a man that lived an abundant life because of his confident trust in God. One day Jabez prayed to the Lord: *"If only you would greatly bless me and increase my territory. May your power go with me to keep me from trouble, so as not to cause me pain." And God granted his request"* (1 Chronicles 4:10, CEB). I believe that God granted his request because the Bible says that Jabez was more honorable than his brothers (1 Chronicles 4:9 NIV). As Jabez prayed, he undoubtedly thought about the unlimited and infinite abundance of God. Jabez became known as a man of prayer. He was not remembered as a great leader, an accurate prophet, or a charismatic preacher. His name is remembered because he operated with an elevated mindset! Jabez prayed bold prayers.

He prayed for:

o God's richest blessings upon himself,
o God to enlarge his territory or property holdings,
o God to be with him, to lift His hand to help him, and for
o God to keep him from evil, from all trouble, harm, and pain.

I believe that God granted his request because his prayer was so bold. Jabez' prayer provides a blueprint to remain honorable, humble, full of faith, and bold (confident in God's ability).

Elevating Your Mind to Rest and Hope

In Acts 2:26, Luke speaks of King David's prophecy: *"Therefore did my heart rejoice, and my tongue was glad; moreover, also my flesh shall rest in hope."* The rest that God provides is not a rest from work, but it is a rest in work. It is not the rest of inactivity.

It is the harmonious working of our affections, will, heart, imagination, and conscience because each has found in God the ideal of its satisfaction and development.[59] In the Message Bible translation of Matthew 11:28-29, Jesus says: *"Are you tired? Worn out? Burned out on religion? Come to me. Get away with me and you'll recover your life. I'll show you how to take a real rest. Walk with me and work with me—watch how I do it. Learn the unforced rhythms of grace."* Jesus invites us to rest because He understands our humanity. In a culture where busyness is the norm, Jesus says, *"Come to Me. Get away with Me and you will recover your life."* God has promised to rebuild, repair, and restore us as His people after whatever hardships or suffering we endure (1 Peter 5:10, KJV). He promises to give us rest and hope.

Elevating our mind to rest and hope is also seen in the following acronym:

- *H*elp
- *O*ver
- *P*roblems
- *E*xpectantly

---

[59] Practical Word Studies In The New Testament, Word Search Bible Software, Version 12, 2012, Accessed December 30, 2019.

When you are expectant, you have an excited feeling that something is about to happen, especially something good. Resting in God leads us to a place of biblical **HOPE**, where we have help over problems expectantly. God's power means He can perform what He says. Psalm 46:1 reads, *"God is our refuge and strength [mighty and impenetrable], A very present and well-proved help in trouble"* (AMP). God's provision means He will provide for us with His best for our eternal good. *"Who provideth for the raven his food? when his young ones cry unto God, they wander for lack of meat."* (Job 38:41). God's protection means He strengthens us and holds us in His hand.

"Fear not, for I am with you; be not dismayed, for I am your God; I will strengthen you, I will help you, I will uphold you with My Righteous Right Hand" (Isaiah 41: 10, ESV). Theologian Matthew Henry paraphrases Isaiah 41:10 in this way:

> *"Fear thou not, for I am with thee, not only within call, but present with thee; be not dismayed at the power of those who are against thee, for I am thy God, and engaged for thee. Art thou weak? I will strengthen thee. Art thou destitute of friends? I will keep thee in a time of need. Art thou ready to sink, ready to fall? I will uphold thee with the right hand of my righteousness."*[60]

We don't have to fear any problems because the Lord Himself is present with His power to provide and protect. Therefore, we can elevate our minds in rest and hope.

---

[60] Pulpit Commentary, Volume 10: Isaiah. Wordsearch Bible 12 Software, 2012. Accessed January 1, 2020.

When we elevate our minds in rest and hope, we can also use God's **HOPE** (help over problems expectantly) to *"be strong in the Lord and in His mighty power... and stand"* (excerpts from Ephesians 6:10, Ephesians 6: 13, NIV). The word strong translates from the original Greek as power, might, and strength. The Lord's mighty power means His Sovereign unlimited power and dominion.[61] The believer must possess power, might, and strength as he walks through the course of this life. This is possible when we know trust in His ability against whatever would oppose us. The believer's strength is not human, or fleshly. The believer's strength is found in the Lord. Elevating our minds to rest and hope is believing that God's **HOPE** (help over problems expectantly) is not a hope-so, it is a know-so! It isn't wishing for the best. It isn't waiting to see what happens and hoping that it turns out well.

Hope is not a feeling or an emotion. Hope is the knowledge of facts. The Christian has a hope that is like faith, a faith that cannot be moved by circumstances or what the eyes see because an unseen God is seen in His faithfulness! When we speak of the attribute of God's faithfulness, it means He is totally trustworthy. He is perfectly faithful, full of faith!

The prophet Jeremiah wrote, *"The Lord's loving kindness indeed never cease, for his compassions never fail. They are new every morning; Great is your faithfulness"* (Lamentations 3:22,23). The biblical definition of hope is *"a confident, favorable, expectation."* Hope is a firm assurance regarding things that are unclear and unknown (Romans 8:24-25; Hebrews 11:1, 7). Hope is a fundamental component of the life of the righteous. Proverbs 23:18 in the Amplified Bible prophesies, *"For surely there is a*

---

[61] Practical Word Studies In The New Testament, Word Search Bible Software, Version 12, 2012, Accessed January 1, 2020.

latter end [a future and a reward], and your hope and expectation shall not be cut off."

Without hope, life loses its meaning and expectation of a better and brighter day. We will conclude the chapter with a review of a story that shows how David handled adversity. From Psalm 28: 1 – 2,

> *"To you I call, O LORD my Rock; do not turn a deaf ear to me. For if you remain silent, I will be like those who have gone down to the pit. Hear my cry for mercy as I call to you for help, as I lift up my hands toward your Most Holy Place."*

For context, Psalm 28 indicates that David prayed this prayer during a life-threatening crisis that threatened not only David but also the entire nation of Israel. David turned to the Lord in desperate times because of who God is, what God can do, and his personal relationship with God. Because of His faithfulness, the Lord was David's *rock*, his sole source of strength, safety, and stability. The distraught king depended on the power of God to deliver him from his enemies.

David elevated his mind over his difficulties and his enemies. He took on a mindset of rest and hope. Although there may be some life situations that will seek to cause us to be afraid, when we stand on the Rock that is Jesus Christ our Lord, the Rock will never tremble under us! (1 Corinthians 10:4, ESV). David had hope because God was his *H.O.P.E.* (*Help Over Problems Expectantly*).

> *Without hope, life loses its meaning and expectation of a better and brighter day.*

As we think about elevating our minds, we must keep the main thing the main thing by thinking on the heavenly instead of the earthly things (Colossians 3:2). We must elevate our minds so that we continually reflect upon the fact that we *"died to this life, and our real life is hidden with Christ in God"* (Colossians 3:3). The real life is in Jesus, who is the main thing!

Principles and Precepts For Transforming Our Thinking

"And do not be conformed to this world [any longer with its superficial values and customs], but be transformed and progressively changed [as you mature spiritually] by the renewing of your mind [focusing on godly values and ethical attitudes], so that you may prove [for yourselves] what the will of God is, that which is good and acceptable and perfect [in His plan and purpose for you]" (Romans 12:2, AMP).

Principle-a universal law that is true in any context, situation, or environment.

Precept-life lessons indicating the way one should act or behave.

Practice-the act of rehearsing a behavior over and over, for the purpose of improving or mastering it.

<u>Chapter 7 Reflection Practices</u>

1. We must know that God is powerful, that He will provide for us, and He will protect us. Jabez prayed bold prayers. He asked for God's richest blessings, more territory, for God's presence and help, and for God to keep him from evil and harm.

   o Think of a situation where your prayers were too small for God. For instance, you could have prayed for help with your rent when God wanted to bless you with a home.
   o How do you really view God?
   o How do your thoughts about God affect your prayer life?

2. Do a thorough assessment of your devotion. Is it really working? Is it changing the way you think? Does your devotion cause your mind to be renewed? How can you improve your devotion?

3. Review the sections on *What Do You Think About Money?* and *Be Intentional and Deliberate About Managing Money.* Make a budget that utilizes the principles and precepts in these sections.

Chapter 8

PATTERNS OF EXCELLENT THINKING

"We are what we repeatedly do. Excellence, then, is not an act, but a habit." – Aristotle

Patterns of Excellent Thinking

A pattern may be defined as, "a series of actions or events that together show how things normally happen or are done." A pattern may also be defined as, "someone or something used as a model to copy; an expected action or repeats in a predictable way."[62]

Your Dictionary.com defines excellent as, "someone or something as exceptional or of high quality, excelling, surpassing, outstandingly good of its kind, of exceptional merit or virtue." Overcoming negative thoughts requires a desire to be a man or woman of exceptional virtue who tirelessly pursues and utilizes a pattern of excellent thinking.

---

[62] https://www.vocabulary.com/dictionary/pattern. Accessed December 14, 2019.

This pursuit is uncommon, but obtainable. Our brains partnered with our minds are incredibly complex, but there is a pattern of expected actions that repeats concerning the way that we think. Science call the pattern of the way we think the Reticular Activating System (RAS). The RAS is a bundle of nerves at our brainstem that filters out unnecessary information, so the important information gets through. Our RAS takes what we focus on and creates a filter for it. It then sifts through the data and presents only the pieces that are important to you. In the same way, the RAS seeks information that validates your beliefs.

It filters the world through the parameters you have given it, which are rooted in your unique life experiences. Our beliefs shape those parameters or reprograms the information that we receive.[63]

> *The Reticular Activating System is simply the gatekeeper of information that is let into our minds.*

The RAS is simply the gatekeeper of information that is let into our minds. Our five senses (sight, hearing, taste, smell and touch) are constantly feeding so much information to our brains that we can't possibly pay attention to all of it. The human body sends 11 million bits per second of information to the brain for processing, yet the conscious mind seems to

---

[63] https://medium.com/desk-of-van-schneider/if-you-want-it-you-might-get-it-the-reticular-activating-system-explained-761b6ac14e53. Accessed December 1, 2019.

be able to process only 50 bits per second.[64] The RAS decides what is important because of the way we have programmed our brains through life which certainly includes patterns of negative thinking. Negative experiences lead to negative thoughts that become memories filed away subconsciously in our minds.

The sub-conscious is, for example, the part of your mind that lets you remember your phone number. Before reading this, you were not conscious (thinking about it right now) of your phone number, but should someone ask you for it, you're able to bring it to the conscious level by pulling the memory of your phone number from your sub-conscious.[65] When you go back to focusing on this book, your mind will put your phone number back into your *sub-conscious* by following the pattern of how we think.[66]

Dreaming and Visualization

Consider the biblical story where Joseph activated his RAS, reprogramed his brain, and created new filters for his conscious thinking by dreaming and visualization.

> *"Now Israel loved Joseph more than all his sons, because he was the son of his old age, and he made him a coat of many colors. But when his brothers saw that their father loved him more than all his brothers, they hated him and could not speak peaceably to him. Now*

---

[64] https://www.britannica.com/science/information-theory/Physiology. Accessed December 1, 2019.

[65] https://painintheenglish.com/case/527/. Accessed December 14, 2019.

[66] IBID. Accessed December 14, 2019.

> *Joseph dreamed a dream, and when he told it to his brothers, they hated him even more. He said to them, "Please listen to this dream which I have dreamed. We were binding sheaves in the field. All of a sudden my sheaf rose up and stood upright, and your sheaves stood around it and bowed down to my sheaf." His brothers said to him, "Will you really reign over us, or will you really have dominion over us?" So they hated him even more because of his dreams and his words. Then he dreamed another dream and told it to his brothers and said, "I have dreamed another dream. The sun and the moon and eleven stars were bowing to me. But when he told it to his father and his brothers, his father rebuked him and said to him,*
>
> *"What is this dream that you have dreamed? Will I and your mother and your brothers really come to bow down ourselves to you to the ground?" So his brothers were jealous of him, but his father kept the matter in mind."* (Genesis 37:3-11, MEV)

Joseph dreamed a dream that became his reality. Although the pathway to the fulfillment of his dream was filled with many hardships, his dream carried him from being sold into slavery by his brothers, to the palace of Pharaoh as second in command of the entire nation of Egypt (Genesis 41:37-40). Joseph was able to describe in detail what he saw in his dream to his brothers and father. He visualized the dream, or he had a vision of his future.

Visualization can be described as the process of using our thoughts to consciously imagine (see) and create that which you intend and desire to experience in your life.

Visualization enables the God-given ability within us to harness the creative power of the mind to change our circumstances and consciously choose the life we create by the way we think, which includes imagining (cognitive), feeling (emotions), and believing (faith).[67]

According to Medical News Today, dreams are stories and images that our minds create while we sleep. They can be entertaining, romantic, and sometimes disturbing or frightening. Furthermore, dreams are a human experience that can be described as a state of consciousness characterized by sensory, cognitive, and emotional occurrences during sleep.[68] The American Sleep Association further states that "dreams can be explained as a succession of sensations, emotions, ideas, and images that occur involuntarily in a person's mind during certain stages of sleep."[69]

Martin Luther King activated his RAS to reprogram his brain from the negative and destructive mindset of his day. He created new filters for his conscious thinking by dreaming and visualization. The "I Have a Dream" speech, before a crowd of some 250,000 people at the 1963 March on Washington, remains one of the most famous speeches in history. Weaving in references to the country's founding fathers and the Bible, King used universal themes to depict the struggles of African

---

[67] https://www.mind-your-reality.com/creative_visualization.html. Accessed December 10, 2019

[68] https://www.medicalnewstoday.com/articles/284378.php. Accessed December 10, 2019.

[69] https://www.sleepassociation.org/about-sleep/dreams/. Accessed December 10, 2019.

Americans, before closing with an improvised sermonic climax of his dreams of equality.[70]

Henry Ford did not invent the car, but he produced an automobile that was within the economic reach of the average American by activating his RAS and the ability of visualization. Ford Motors sold more cars and transformed the automobile from a luxury toy to a mainstay of American society.[71]

By unquestionable belief and persistent determination in his dream, in 1899 Henry Ford formed the Detroit Automobile Company, which quickly failed after only a few vehicles were produced. Further discouragement occurred in 1902 when Ford was dismissed by his board of directors because of his inability to bring a car to production. In October of 1908 Henry Ford proclaimed, "I will build a motor car for the great multitude," and because of his dream, he did just that. In the 19 years of the Model T's existence, Henry Ford built more than 15 million cars and they were sold around the world.

Henry Ford realized his dream of producing an automobile that was reasonably priced, reliable, and efficient with the introduction of the Model T in 1908.[72] By activating his RAS, Ford reprogramed his brain from the opposing, negative experiences of failure and a dis-believing mindset of his day.

Ford created new filters for his conscious thinking by dreaming and visualization of his Model T automobile, changing the world forever. This is a pattern for excellent thinking! Our RAS validates what we believe. Joseph believed

---

[70] https://www.history.com/topics/civil-rights-movement/i-have-a-dream-speech. Accessed December 15, 2019.
[71] http://www.eyewitnesstohistory.com/ford.htm. Accessed December 14, 2019.
[72] http://hfha.org/the-ford-story/henry-ford-an-impact-felt/. Accessed December 14, 2019.

his dream and he visualized a future that became reality in his life. On April 4, 2019, Martin Luther King Jr. was killed by an assassin's bullet in Memphis.

The world has changed greatly since 1968 when Dr. King was assassinated, but Dr. King's dream survives in the fabric of our society. Dr. King visualized a brighter future for all of America's citizens.

Henry Ford had a dream and visualized the building of an affordable automobile and because of his dream by 1923 the company was producing more than half of America's automobiles; and, by the end of the 1920s, Ford had more than 20 overseas assembly plants in Europe, Latin America, Canada, Asia, South Africa, and Australia.[73]

> *By activating the Reticular Activating System, Martin Luther King and Henry Ford achieved what others could not.*

The emphasis of this section is to understand that biologically God has built and wired our RAS to filter the world's information through the parameters we have given our brains. The filtering takes place through our unique life experiences. As God's people, faith and belief are a part of this equation. What we have faith in and believe in through life experiences (good, bad, negative, or positive) shapes and frames our world.

---

[73] https://www.britannica.com/topic/Ford-Motor-Company. Accessed December 15, 2019.

Faith and Understanding Frames Our World

Hebrews 11:3 professes, *"Through faith we understand that the worlds were framed by the word of God, so that things which are seen were not made of things which do appear."* This scripture models a pattern of excellent thinking. God's Word provides the guidelines for activating the RAS, to reprogram our brains, and create new filters for our minds and how we think. Using Hebrews 11:3, the pattern for excellent thinking has three components: faith, understanding, and framed by the Word of God.

Faith. Chosen as God's people, we are members of an incredible heritage and legacy of faith by which to cultivate excellent thinking. The entire chapter of Hebrews 11 creates new filters for our thinking when we consider what God has done and will continue to do through men and women of faith. We will discuss a few of the verses in Hebrews 11 from in the Message Bible:

o **Verse 4: Faith moved Abel** *to choose a more acceptable sacrifice to offer God than his brother Cain, and God declared him righteous because of his offering **of faith**.*

We must shift our thinking concerning our motives when we offer sacrifices to God. Abel gave a bloody sacrifice from his animal stock. This sacrifice was not pretty. It was symbolic of the sacrifice of Jesus, which required total submission to God. Cain gave fruit from the soil, which did not require blood. Although the fruit was pretty, there was no blood.

A pattern of excellent thinking declares, *"I will not give God what does not cause or call for a sacrifice."*

o **Verse 7: Faith opened Noah's heart** *to receive revelation and warnings from God about what was coming, even things that had never been seen. But he stepped out in reverent obedience to God and built an ark that would save him and his family.*

When Noah built the ark, he had never seen an ark. When he warned of rain, they had never experienced rain. A pattern of excellent thinking allows you to receive witty innovations from God! A pattern of excellent thinking declares, *"I will follow God's instructions, even in unfamiliar territory."*

o **Verse 27: Holding faith's promise** *Moses abandoned Egypt and had no fear of Pharaoh's rage because he persisted in faith...*

Moses grew up in Pharaoh's home. Pharaoh had the power to destroy Moses with a single command. By faith, Noah turned his back on his upbringing and challenged Pharaoh. A pattern of excellent thinking will cause you to challenge your upbringing and confront things that need to be changed. *"Do not act as if you had ten thousand years to throw away. Be good for something while you live, and it is in your power."* – Marcus Aurelius

Understanding. Hebrews 11:3 tells us that faith causes us to understand. Understanding means to "perceive with the mind, to know a true fact, to gain insight."[74] Faith itself gives us a perceptive mind, the ability to know a true fact and gain

---

[74] Wordsearch Bible Software, 2012, Mounce's Complete Expository Dictionary of Old and New Testament Words: Expository Dictionary. Accessed December 17, 2019.

insight. One of the areas in which faith gives us a perceptive mind is in the matter of creation.

Faith helps us to perceive that the Word of God is the catalyst and initiator of creation. John's Gospel records:

> *"In the beginning the Word already existed. The Word was with God, and the Word was God. He existed in the beginning with God. God created everything through Him, and nothing was created except through him. The Word gave life to everything that was created, and his life brought light to everyone. The light shines in the darkness, and the darkness can never extinguish it."* (John 1:1-5, NLT)

Understanding that Jesus Christ was preexistent simply means that He was there before creation. He has always existed. In the beginning does not mean *from* the beginning. Jesus Christ was already there. He did not become, He was not created, and He never had a beginning. He *"was in the beginning with God"* (John 17:5; John 8:58). Was, in the original Greek, is the word often used for deity.

It means *"to be"* or *"I am"*. To be means "continuous existence, without beginning or origin."[75]

Framed by the Word of God. In Hebrews 11:3, to be framed means "to complete, to prepare, put in order, restore for a specific purpose."[76] As the world was created and framed by Jesus as the Word of God, we as God's people are capable of framing our world by the Word of God! For example,

---

[75] Wordsearch Bible, Preacher's Outline and Sermon Bible - Commentary - John, 2012. Accessed December 17, 2019
[76] Mounce's Complete Expository Dictionary of Old and New Testament Words: Expository Dictionary. Accessed December 17, 2019.

the principles and precepts of Psalm 91 provide us with a pattern of excellent thinking that many applied during the COVID-19 pandemic of 2020. The Contemporary English Version encourages us:

"Live under the protection of God Most High and stay in the shadow of God All-Powerful. Then you will say to the LORD, "You are my fortress, my place of safety; you are my God, and I trust you." The Lord will keep you safe from secret traps and deadly diseases. He will spread his wings over you and keep you secure.

His faithfulness is like a shield or a city wall. You won't need to worry about dangers at night or arrows during the day. And you won't fear diseases that strike in the dark or sudden disaster at noon. You will not be harmed, though thousands fall all around you. And with your own eyes you will see the punishment of the wicked. The LORD Most High is your fortress. Run to him for safety, and no terrible disasters will strike you or your home. God will command his angels to protect you wherever you go. They will carry you in their arms, and you won't hurt your feet on the stones. You will overpower the strongest lions and the most deadly snakes.

The Lord says, If you love me and truly know who I am, I will rescue you and keep you safe. When you are in trouble, call out to me. I will answer and be there to protect and honor you. You will live a long life and see my saving power."

Thinking like God thinks is to know that your life is beneath the shelter and shadow of His wings! Psalm 91 speaks of God's power, presence, intentions, safety, and protection. God is our life's fortress, protecting and delivering us from deadly diseases. With the Lord as our refuge, nothing will be able to affect or infect us that will diminish God's plans and purposes for our lives. We frame and shape our world by God's Word! As God's people we don't have to worry about anything.

The way that we respond to threats, such as COVID-19, becomes a catalyst for fear or faith about the future.

During the pandemic, people were asking questions such as: How long do I quarantine my family if we believe we have symptoms? What about my job? How long will we be impacted by this pandemic? Will our food supply run out? Is it safe to travel? These are all valid questions that should be addressed, but we should remain in peace. God's peace will help us to establish a pattern for excellent thinking even in the midst of a global pandemic!

God's attributes of creating and shaping are essential qualities that make Him uniquely God. They define and are the source of His actions. As noted in Hebrews 11:3 and John 1:1-5, the purpose of God's actions was to create! When we activate our faith and believe that we have the ability and capability to frame and shape our world, God says, *"You have seen well, for I am alert and active, watching over My word to perform it"* (Jeremiah 1:12 AMP).

God is saying that your visualizations and faith are working! By the authority and warranty of God's Word, believing activates our RAS, reprogramming our brains, creating new filters, and creating excellent patterns of thinking!

The Model of Excellent Thinking in Philippians 4:8

No study of overcoming negative thinking is complete without a look at Paul's admonishment to the church at Philippi. In the English Standard version of Philippians 4:8, Paul gives the blueprint on how to think:

> *"Finally, brothers, whatever is true, whatever is honorable, whatever is just, whatever is pure, whatever is lovely, whatever is commendable, if there is any excellence, if there is anything worthy of praise, think about these things."*

Think truth. Truth is timeless, applicable for today and the future. Many things in the world seem to be true, but they are not.

They are false and deceptive, an illusion, and a counterfeit. We are to keep our minds upon things that are true. Jesus proclaimed, *"I am the way, the truth, and the life. No one can come to the Father except through me"* (John 14:6). Jesus is the source of truth, the perfect standard of what is right. He is the reality of all God's promises. Jesus as the **truth never changes!** This is the type of truth that Paul wants us to think about. Keep thinking about these things!

Think honor. Honor in the Bible means "esteem, value, or great respect." The Apostle Peter tells us to *"honor all people, love the brotherhood, fear God, honor the king"* (1 Peter 2:17). We honor those in authority (the king) because they represent God's ultimate authority. A classic example is the command to *"submit to the governing authorities because they have been* *established by God"* (Romans 13:1-6). Paul further encourages the church at Rome to *"love each other with genuine affection and take delight in honoring each other"* (Romans 12:10). Giving honor is better than receiving honor.

As Christians, we honor people because they have been created in God's image. As we honor others, we honor the Lord. Keep thinking on these things!

Think justice (fairness). *"The Lord demands fairness in every business deal; He sets the standard"* (Proverbs 16:11). God expects fairness from us. Whether we buy or sell, make a product or offer a service, we must govern ourselves in honesty. No amount of rationalizing can cover up a dishonest business practice. Honesty and fairness are not always easy, but it is what God demands. All of us want to be treated fairly, but do we treat others fairly? Only as the Lord governs our hearts can we learn to be as fair in our treatment of others as we expect others to be toward us. Keep thinking about these things!

Think purity. God wants us to be pure. The word pure in the original Greek means "not contaminated."[77]

God's desire is for us to clean up our behavior when we begin a new life with Him. As we live our new life in Christ, we do not want to live as Jesus saw the Pharisees in Matthew 23:25, *"How terrible it will be for you teachers of religious law and you Pharisees. Hypocrites! You are so careful to clean the outside of the cup and the dish, but inside you are filthy—full of greed and self-indulgence!"* In other words, true purity comes from the heart. The Pharisees were meticulous about the details of ceremonial cleanliness, but they had lost their perspective on inner purity. Daily application of God's Word has a purifying

---

[77] Practical Word Studies in the New Testament. Wordsearch Bible 12 Software, Retrieved December 7, 2019.

effect, removing the contaminated influence of the world on our mind and heart. The Lord cleanses us by the *"washing of His word"* (Ephesians 5:26). Keep thinking about these things!

Think acceptable (lovely). The word acceptable may be translated as "pleasing, agreeable, lovely; things that excite love."[78]

To excite is to "stimulate, animate, or energize."[79] Winning millions of dollars in a sweepstakes will definitely excite you! Flowers are pleasing to many. The sun setting on a warm summer's evening is certainly lovely. However, the Bible tells us that *"nothing in all creation will ever be able to separate us from the love of God that is revealed in Christ Jesus our Lord"* (Romans 8:39). God's love is beyond measure! No matter what happens to us, no matter where we are, we can never be lost to His love that is able to reach us and heal us. Believers have always had to face hardships such as persecution, illness, imprisonment, and even death. These life experiences can cause fear to arise and feelings of abandonment by the Lord. But Paul exclaims that it is *impossible* to be separated from Christ! His death for us is proof of his unconquerable love. Now that is acceptable! Keep thinking on these things!

Think commendable (good report). We live in a very toxic world. Many nutritionists recommend that we need to detox our bodies at least three to four times a year. From this perspective, how often do we *detox our minds*? As stated earlier in the book, over half of our daily thoughts are negative! So, it is imperative that we detox our minds.

---

[78] IBID, Retrieved December 7, 2019.

[79] https://www.vocabulary.com/dictionary/excite. Accessed December 7, 2019.

How often do you detox your mind?

It is impossible to not be affected and impacted by the toxicity of the world. This may cause many to enter the church or workplace pessimistic, sarcastic, rude, or downright difficult. These attitudes potentially create a negative environment that becomes filled with irritation, frustration, and vexation of the mind that impacts everyone. A detox of the mind will help to create a better, more productive organizational environment.

We can start by thinking on whatever is commendable, that which is "admirable; *well-spoken of,* things of the highest quality." If you encounter someone who may not even be aware that their mind needs a detox, speak well of them and express some form of admiration. This will deposit a seed of esteem. Try commending with these seeds:

o We love what you do for our organization every day. You motivate and help to solve problems. You truly are a valuable team player.
o Your people skills make you an invaluable team member. We need more people like you!
o Your ability to listen to others' ideas with concern and an open mind creates an environment of mutual respect where relationships are healthy and growing making our environment better!
o You've got a winner's attitude! No problem is too complex to solve, no mountain too high to climb, and we love your example.

The Message Bible translation of 1 Corinthians 3:6-7 reads *"I planted the seed, Apollos watered the plants, but God made you grow. It's not the one who plants or the one who waters who is at the center of this process but God, who makes things grow."*

> **When we express admiration and speak well of one another, seeds of esteem and appreciation are planted into the minds of others.**

We can plant seeds of kind words and affirmations that God will cause to grow. Keep thinking about these things!

Think excellence (virtue). Luke 10:27 provides a tremendous example of excellent or virtuous thinking.

"You shall love the Lord your God with all your heart, with all your soul, with all your strength, and with all your mind, and your neighbor as yourself" (NKJV). If love is authentic, there has to be a *demonstration so it can* be seen and understood. To love our neighbors is a demonstration of our love for God. To love your neighbor as yourself, you must first love yourself. Loving yourself starts with liking yourself, which is only possible if you respect yourself. You will never be able to fully respect yourself if you don't think about yourself like God thinks about you! How does God think of you? God thinks of you like He thinks of Jesus: *"This is my Son, chosen and marked by my love, the delight of my life"* (Matthew 3:17, MSG). Keep thinking on these things!

> **You will never be able to fully respect yourself if you don't think about yourself like God thinks about you!**

Think praise. According to the Online Etymology Dictionary, the word praise comes from the Latin *pretium,* which is "price," or "value." Praise may be defined generally as an ascription of value or worth.[80] The King James Version of the Bible uses the word praise 222 times in the Old Testament and 26 in the New Testament. One example of praise includes Nehemiah 8, where 50,000 - 60,000 of God's people gathered for a praise service.[81] The Lord had freed them from Babylonian captivity and enabled them to rebuild the wall of Jerusalem in just 52 days. He also helped them to rebuild their homes. Praise invites God's presence. *"He inhabits the praises of His people"* (Psalm 22:3). When we reflect upon praise, praise gets our focus off ourselves and back on God. In our "selfie" focused world, we need the constant reminder that "It's All About Him!"

> **When we reflect upon praise, it brings us to a place of humility, where we remember our dependency on God.**

---

[80] https://www.etymonline.com/word/praise. Accessed December 18, 2019.

[81] Preachers Outline and Sermon Bible, Wordsearch 12 Bible Software 2012, Accessed December 18, 2019.

When we reflect upon praise, praise becomes a defense and defeats the enemy! *"As they began to sing and praise, the Lord set ambushes against the men of Ammon and Moab and Mount Seir who were invading Judah, and they were defeated"* (2 Chronicles 20:22). When we reflect upon praise, praise changes us. Sometimes God doesn't just change our situations, He changes our hearts! *"Create in me a clean heart, O God; and renew a right spirit within me"* (Psalm 51:10). Keep thinking about these things!

Keep Thinking About These Things

From the original Greek, to keep thinking about these things means "to think about; to think on; to let one's mind dwell on; to calculate; to evaluate; to consider, reflect, reason, and ponder."[82] Paul's message in Philippians 4: 8 tells us to focus our thoughts until they shape our behavior. What we think about is what we do and become because thoughts shape our behavior. Our minds are immensely powerful. Yet, most of us probably spend little time reflecting on the way we think.

> *Most of us probably spend little time reflecting on the way we think. After all, who thinks about thinking?*

---

[82] IBID, Retrieved December 7, 2019.

After all, who thinks about thinking? However, the way we think about ourselves turns into our reality. What we think directly influences how we feel and how we behave. If you think you're a failure, you'll feel like a failure. Then, you'll act like a failure, which reinforces your belief that you *must be* a failure.

Just because you think something, doesn't make it true. We can alter our perceptions and change our lives by training our minds to think like God thinks. There are two sources of our thinking: God or the devil. Speaking to an audience of Pharisees, Jesus rebukes them:

> *"You belong to your father, the devil, and you want to carry out your father's desire. He was a murderer from the beginning, not holding to the truth, for there is no truth in him. When he lies, he speaks his native language, for he is a liar and the father of lies. Yet because I tell the truth, you do not believe me! Can any of you prove me guilty of sin? If I am telling the truth, why don't you believe me? He who belongs to God hears what God says. The reason you do not hear is that you do not belong to God."* (John 8:44-47, NIV)

When negative thoughts come to our minds, we don't have to believe the lies of the devil! When we walk in the Truth that is Jesus Christ, the devil is defeated, and God is exalted in every aspect of our lives! A mindset governed by the world and the flesh is what leads to anxiety, worry, emptiness, and restlessness because there is no trust in God. We must consider and reflect upon the Sovereignty of God so that our minds are renewed. This pattern of excellent thinking insulates us from a worldly mindset. A mind that is saturated in the reality of God's sovereignty does not have to be worry about anything. Keep thinking about these things!

A Pattern of Godly Influence: Character, Capability, and Competency

There is a definition of influence that I have used in leadership training for many years. Influence is *"the capacity to become a compelling and irresistible force that affects the actions, behavior, and conduct of others."*

When we are notified that a hurricane or a tornado is coming our way, we recognize that the force and power of the winds that will soon arrive are an irresistible, unstoppable force. Therefore, we will go to the grocery store and we will stock up on food supplies, water, and batteries. Many will purchase a portable generator in anticipation of a power outage. The news of the tornado affects our actions and our behavior.

Similarly, godly influence is a compelling, irresistible force that affects the actions, behavior, and conduct of others. A person endowed with godly character, capabilities and competencies becomes an irresistible and unstoppable force that affects the behavior of all within their sphere of influence. Consider the chart below. As you move from left to right, note that life and ministry infused by godly influence begins with character. Now start with the first column and move up and down from top to bottom.

Character is the center of your **being** and the **heart** is a synonym for character. *"For as he thinks in his heart, so is he..."* (Proverbs 23:7, NIV). Your heart determines your character.

Character	Capabilities	Competencies
Being	Becoming	Doing
Heart	Head	Hand

Capabilities describe the potential or quality that grants the drive and ability to learn and acquire new skills for a given task or assignment. We can also view capabilities as abilities which are not yet developed. From the second column, your capabilities speak of what and who you are becoming, which is a persistent and continual process of change. This process is determined by what's in your head, which represents what and how you think. Our thinking can be positive or negative in the process of becoming.

Competencies can include a combination of knowledge, basic requirements (capabilities), skills, abilities, behavior, and attitudes. Competence is possessing skills and knowledge that allow you to complete an assignment successfully and proficiently. Competence denotes being qualified and experienced. As we move to the third column. Competence is the place of doing with your hands.

What you and I can do ultimately determines our competency level. *"And whatsoever ye do, do it heartily, as to the Lord, and not unto men"* (Colossians 3:23). Competence is a result of improved capabilities obtained through the process of becoming, a process that begins and ends in character development. In other words, if I start with Godly character in my process to becoming, then I can improve my capabilities and consequently become competent. If we have the character of Jesus Christ as the core of our being, then we obtain the mind of Christ, which transforms our capabilities in what and how we think as we become.

Therefore, our thinking governs our competencies (what we do). When we have the mind of Christ, we do things *valiantly* and *virtuously*. Valiantly can be translated in the original Hebrew as "virtuous capability." How do we do things valiantly and virtuously? This is accomplished by developing and enhancing the heart (the character of God), the head (the capabilities possessed when we think like God thinks), and the hand (the competencies of God). We perform valiantly when we reinforce truth that renews the minds of those that are a part of our sphere of influence. This is a pattern of excellent thinking!

A Model of Influence from the Apostle Paul

The Apostle Paul's character, capabilities, and competencies were an "irresistible, compelling force that affected the actions, behavior, and conduct" of believers in his day and today. In Ephesians 4:22-24, his message is a personal call to change your life, habits, and character.

God does not want us to alter a few things; He wants us to put off the old man as you would remove a garment:

> *"That ye put off concerning the former conversation the old man, which is corrupt according to the deceitful lusts; And be renewed in the spirit of your mind; And that ye put on the new man, which after God is created in righteousness and true holiness."*

This change (putting off the old man and putting on the new) aims to bring the mind under the government of truth by the Lordship of Jesus Christ. When Jesus becomes Lord of our lives, He must also become Lord and governor of our minds. When we put on the new, we must become tenaciously focused on being spiritually minded, as one who has been given a holy nature and an incorruptible new life. The new self is a person that is in fellowship with God, obedient to God's will, and devoted to God's service.

When He becomes the Lord and governor of our minds, we can repeatedly build character, improve capabilities, and master competencies. Then we become "an irresistible, compelling force that affects, the actions, behavior and conduct of others." This is Godly influence. This is a pattern of excellent thinking!

> *"We are what we repeatedly do. Excellence, then, is not an act, but a habit."* Aristotle

Principles and Precepts for Transforming Our Thinking

"And do not be conformed to this world [any longer with its superficial values and customs], but be transformed and progressively changed [as you mature spiritually] by the renewing of your mind [focusing on godly values and ethical attitudes], so that you may prove [for yourselves] what the will of God is, that which is good and acceptable and perfect [in His plan and purpose for you]" (Romans 12:2, AMP).

Principle-a universal law that is true in any context, situation, or environment.

Precept-life lessons indicating the way one should act or behave.

Practice-the act of rehearsing a behavior over and over, for the purpose of improving or mastering it.

Chapter 8 Reflection Practices

1. Nutritionists recommend that you detox your body three to four times a year. We must also detox our minds, renewing our minds daily. Using the principles and precepts in this chapter, how can you improve your daily devotion to be sure that you are detoxing your mind? Consider implementing some of the suggestions below.

   o Start reading scriptures related to your areas of struggle (financial, depression, anger, frustration, etc.)
   o Frame your world by building your faith and gaining understanding. Purposely filter out negativity in your environment by using the principles and precepts we discussed from Philippians 4:8 and Hebrews 11.
   o Practice commendations that plant seeds of esteem. Deliberately affirm that difficult family member, church member, or coworker.

2. Ask God to give you dreams about your purpose. Take action to develop your character, capabilities, and competencies related to that purpose. For instance, you can enroll in a college course or intentionally improve your attitude.

Chapter 9

IT IS WHAT IT IS BUT IT IS NOT WHAT IT COULD BE

"You could leave life right now. Let that determine what you do and say and think."

Marcus Aurelius

The expression "it is what it is" was voted *USA Today's* number one cliché in 2004.[83] For some, the phrase means "it's not going to change, so get over it already!" This interpretation is deep in the well of negative thinking. This mindset suggests that the situation appears to be beyond change so accept it as it is because that's life. Many hold to this negative outlook or pattern of life. However, Orville and Wilbur Wright believed differently. They thought, *"It is not what it could be!"* They had a God perspective of the future.

---

[83] https://guff.com/this-is-what-the-phrase-it-is-what-it-is-really-means. Accessed November 29, 2019.

It Is What It Is but It Is *Not* What It Could Be

In the late 1890s and early 1900s, Orville and Wilbur Wright lived within an "it is what it is" world concerning airplanes and flight. They were the sons of Milton Wright, a Bishop of the United Brethren in Christ. In their early years the two boys helped their father, who edited a journal called the *Religious Telescope*. Later, they began a paper of their own, *West Side News*. They went into business together printing everything from religious handouts to commercial fliers. Orville and Wilbur later became bicycle mechanics, an occupation that prepared them for their future.

When the brothers took up the problems of flight, they had a solid grounding in practical mechanics (knowledge of how to build machines).[84] History records Wilbur saying, "From the time we were little children, my brother Orville and myself lived together, worked together, and in fact, thought together." Orville Wright once stated, "If birds can glide for long periods of time, then... why can't I?"[85] The Wright brothers lived at a time of incredible skepticism and disbelief concerning man's ability to fly, but they thought, "If we worked on the assumption that what is accepted as true really is true, then there would be little hope for advance."[86] The Wright brothers were also quoted as saying, "We believe in a good God, a bad Devil, and a hot Hell, and more than anything else we

---

[84] https://www.notablebiographies.com/We-Z/Wright-Brothers.html. Accessed November 29, 2019.

[85] https://thewrightbrothersandben.weebly.com/quotes.html. Accessed November 29, 2019.

[86] Bellis, Mary. "Quotes of the Wright Brothers." ThoughtCo, Aug. 31, 2019, thoughtco.com/famous-quotes-of-the-wright-brothers-1992679.

believed that same God did not intend man should ever fly."[87] They did not subscribe to "It is what it is!" Through skepticism (perhaps even their own), disbelief around the world, and no financial backing in the initial stages, the Wright brothers chose to believe that things could be different.

They believed "it is not what it could be" concerning their current situation.[88] Their Bible-filled upbringing mandated that faith had to undoubtedly come alive.

Faith Silences the Negative Influence of *"It Is What It Is"*

Influence is a cognitive factor that tends to have an effect on what we do. Influence may further be defined as having an effect on the nature, behavior, development, action, or thoughts of a matter."[89] We don't know for certain, but I believe that their father Bishop Wright preached several Sunday-morning messages from Hebrews 11: 1 that influenced his sons. These sermons silenced the resident voice that whispered, "It is what it is!" in their heads and in their hearts.

In the phrase *"faith is the substance of things hoped for,"* the writer shows the operative and practical sense of faith. Faith undergirds or supports what we hope for. The word substance

---

[87] https://www.goodreads.com/work/quotes/42099162-the-wright-brothers. Accessed November 29, 2019.

[88] https://www.baltimoresun.com/opinion/op-ed/bs-ed-thomas-wright-bros-20150606-story.html. Accessed November 30, 2019.

[89] https://www.yourdictionary.com/influence. Accessed November 30, 2019.

literally means *"a standing under."*[90] Amplified a bit further, substance is that which though unseen, exists beneath what is visible. Substance carries the meaning of a foundation. The foundation of a building is unseen, but the building above ground is seen. The foundation is real and present, supporting the building that stands in clear view, but it is unseen. Likewise, faith is the foundation for what we hope for and the foundation for our relationship with God. Faith is the very beginning of everything that matters. In its simplest form, faith is merely belief.

When we begin to put faith to work, it becomes confidence. In its best form, when it becomes fully operational, faith is trust.

Faith (belief), confidence and trust are all a portion of the substance that became the pattern for the Wright brothers' success against all odds. Faith as the substance of things hoped for, coupled with confidence and trust in God is the pattern that silences the negative thoughts and the influence of the "it is what it is" mindset. Faith reveals what could be. The Wright brothers knew that the flight industry was not what it could be. To change it, they applied their faith and allowed God to show them what it could be. I wonder what their mindset was while they waited on God.

Do you find it challenging to wait upon the promises of God? While you wait, how do you prevent an "it is what it is" attitude? In chapter one, *God Is Always Thinking About Us*, we discussed the power of reflective thinking.

Recall that reflective thinking is a practical tool for shifting our thinking away from the negative to the positive. Reflective

---

[90] Vines Expository Dictionary of Old and New Testament Words. Wordsearch Bible 12 Software, Retrieved November 29, 2019.

thinking helps us to think like God thinks and overcome negative thinking.

As we reflect on God's character and patiently wait while He is working, the influence of "it is what it is" is silenced as we focus on the fact that God will give us solutions that we have never even imagined. "But as it is written: *Eye has not seen, nor ear heard, nor have entered into the heart of man the things which God has prepared for those who love Him*" (1 Corinthians 2:9, NKJV). This does not mean we can completely stop negative thoughts from coming to us, but adopting the mindset described in this section cultivates and strengthens the pattern of excellent thinking. We must constantly have a mindset of reset.

> *We cannot completely stop negative thoughts, but we must constantly have a mindset of reset where we demand and command our minds to return to the positive.*

A Mindset of Reset: Think What It Could Be

The most important thing to understand and remember about the past is just that, it's in the past. There is nothing that we can do about yesterday. Yesterday has gone on into history with its memories, successes, and even our failures. Vince Lombardi, the former coach of the NFL's Green Bay Packers, once told his team, *"Perfection is not attainable, but if we chase perfection, we can catch excellence."* He also told them that "the difference between a successful person and others is not a lack of strength, not a lack of knowledge, but rather a lack of will."[91]

Chasing excellence in our thinking is also a matter of our will and determination that requires constant reset. The Amplified Version of Acts 3:19-20 gives us instruction on how to let go of the past and create a mindset of reset.

> *"So repent (change your mind and purpose); turn around and return [to God], that your sins may be erased (blotted out, wiped clean), that times of refreshing (of recovering from the effects of heat, of reviving with fresh air) may come from the presence of the Lord. And that He may send [to you] the Christ (the Messiah), Who before was designated and appointed for you."*

The term refresh means "to be made new, renewed, readjusted, changed, or turned around" in the original Greek. In addition, to refresh is "to give intermission from labor, to give rest, to cause to cease."[92] Jesus renewed, refreshed, and changed the mind (thoughts) of a man that was possessed in the town of Gadara. The demon possessed man went from dwelling in tombs, naked, cutting himself, and constantly crying out to sitting and clothed in his *right mind* (Mark 5:1-13).

Jesus activated a mindset of reset for this man who had been tormented with thousands of demons that wanted to destroy his life. The reset facilitated a change in the man's

---

[91] https://www.goalcast.com/2018/05/30/vince-lombardi-quotes-appreciate-excellence/. Accessed November 30, 2019.
[92] Practical Word Studies in The New Testament. Wordsearch Bible Software, Version 12. Accessed November 30, 2019.

past condition, reprogrammed the filters of his thinking, and initiated his ability to think like God thinks.

Technology has provided us with filters to purify our water. We also change the filters in our heating and AC units to keep the air clean. In the same manner, it will always be necessary to filter our thoughts concerning what and how we think about ourselves based on past experiences. To reset means "to be set again." Does your mind need to be reset? Every time a bowler knocks down the pins, they are automatically reset so that he can continue the game. This process occurs over and over as long as the bowler is in the game. And if for whatever reason the pins do not automatically reset, the bowler can request help from an attendant by pressing the reset button.

As long as we are in the game of life, we will have to *reset our mindset*. When you find it challenging to overcome negative thinking, you can ask God to help you to have a mindset of reset. *"Forget about what's happened; don't keep going over old history. Be alert, be present. I'm about to do something brand-new"* (Isaiah 43:18, MSG). Having a mindset of reset helps us to reprogram our thinking so that we think of what it could be. Change the filter of your thinking and see yourself getting a promotion on your job with a significant pay increase. See and visualize yourself getting the house you want. See yourself finally writing the book that is in you. See yourself overcoming that anger. By visualizing God's new thing, we can see ourselves in the plans of God. We can see ourselves in the future that God has destined for us.

The writer of Hebrews reminds us, *"You need endurance, so that after you have done God's will, you can receive what he has promised.*

For in a very little while the One who is coming will return—He will not delay; but my righteous one will live by faith..." (Hebrews 10:36-38, ISV). Endurance gives us the ability to keep doing something that is difficult or challenging, possessing the strength to last. When we have endurance, we continually release our faith and remain steadfast and unmovable. Through this process, we are training our minds to change the filter of our thinking. A mindset of reset also reminds me not to compare myself with others. Paul reminds the Corinthians:

> *"We do not dare to put ourselves in the same group with those who think that they are very important. We do not compare ourselves to them. They use themselves to measure themselves, and they judge themselves by what they themselves are. This shows that they know nothing."*

> (2 Corinthians 10:12, ICB)

When we compare ourselves to others, we look in the wrong mirror. We should be a reflection of God, not other people. A mindset of reset, thinking about what it could be, reminds me to say to myself, "Oh there I am, I'm made in the image and likeness of God and I've been looking for me!" (Genesis 1:27). When I wake up in the morning, I see myself as God sees me because if I think like He thinks, then I will see what He sees!

> *You can see yourself as God views you if you think like He thinks. If you think like God thinks, then you will see what God sees.*

A Mindset of Reset: Think Before You Speak

With a mindset of reset, we *"think the same way that Christ Jesus thought"* (Philippians 2:5, CEV). Jesus' thinking was grounded in His relationship with His Father as seen in John 13: 49-50 (NIV):

> *"For I did not speak on my own, but the Father who sent me commanded me to say all that I have spoken. I know that his command leads to eternal life. So whatever I say is just what the Father has told me to say."*

What we say is always a result of what we think. Scientists have proven that it takes just 600 milliseconds, for the human brain to think of a word, apply the rules of grammar to it, and send it to the mouth to be spoken! [93] Thinking before we speak is an important practical and spiritual skill to master for all kinds of situations.

It can improve our relationships with other people, and it enables us to express ourselves in a more effective manner.

---

[93] https://www.livescience.com/5780-speed-thought-speech-traced-brain.html. Accessed January 15, 2020.

Most people love to speak, but we can get carried away sometimes! The Amplified Version of James 1:19 admonishes us to be slow to speak.

> *"Understand this, my beloved brothers and sisters. Let everyone be quick to hear [be a careful, thoughtful listener], slow to speak [a speaker of carefully chosen words and], slow to anger [patient, reflective, forgiving] ..."*

Listening to others is important because it shows honor and respect. Being quick to hear affects how we maintain personal relationships, gain the knowledge needed to complete a job, take notes in a class, or figure out which bus to take to the airport. It's more than hearing the words that are directed at us; listening is an active process by which we make sense of, assess, and respond to what we hear. To think like God thinks, our hearing must begin by hearing the Word of God, which is the foundation of faith (Romans 1:17, ISV). Listening to the Word of the Lord is vital because the Word is the bedrock of instruction for life and ministry. This further means that as God's people we must be willing to listen to God's perspective instead of speaking our own ideas.

Consider the story of Job and the conversation with his friends in Job 32 where they discuss his suffering. Listening to the conversation, Elihu stood by in the crowd. As he listened to the discussion of Job's case, he became convinced that he understood the reason for Job's affliction. Elihu was angered because he believed Job and his friends spoke inaccurately about God. Further study of the passage reveals that Elihu displayed an arrogant attitude. He claimed that God's Spirit had given him wisdom as opposed to his elders, whom he was suggesting lacked the wisdom of God.

I have no doubt that Elihu's intent was good, but what he spoke was not God. Elihu did not think before he spoke. Jesus promises us that the Holy Spirit will teach us all things and remind of us everything (John 14:26). As we hear or listen to the voice of God through the ongoing ministry of the Holy Spirit, we cultivate our ability to think like God thinks. The Holy Spirit will remind us of everything that God has taught us.

When we follow the direction of the Holy Spirit, our speech becomes what we have heard from Him and then we can represent Him well. Before we speak, we must think like God thinks! To think like God thinks is to say what Jesus said and Jesus always said what His Father commanded Him to say because He wanted to please Him! (John 13:49; John 8:28-30, NIV).

A Mindset of Reset: You Are A Kingdom Citizen

With a mindset of reset, we practice forgetting things from the past and we continuously press forward (Philippians 3:13). We let go of things that we did not get right, things that we did not say right, failures and flops, and disappointments. The goal before us must be a pursuit to live in heavenly places while here on earth as described in Ephesians 2:4-6:

> *"But God, who is rich in mercy, because of His great love with which He loved us, even when we were dead in trespasses, made us alive together with Christ (by grace you have been saved), and raised us up together,*

and made us sit together in the heavenly places in Christ Jesus."

As Christians we live in two worlds; we are residents of two realms. We are citizens of our home cities and countries with a physical street address, but we are also Kingdom citizens and you must have a Kingdom mindset. We must know that we are seated next to the one who created the world (John 1:1-3).

A Mindset of Reset: Pursue Righteousness

Righteousness is defined as "the condition of being acceptable to God as made possible by God."[94] God's standard of righteousness is what defines true righteousness and there is nothing that we can ever do to make ourselves righteousness through our own deeds and conduct. Proverbs 21:21 in the NIV says, *"He who pursues righteousness and love finds life, prosperity and honor."*

Life. The Hebrew word for life in this passage carries the meaning of preserving life. When we pursue righteousness, the reward is a preservation of the life that God has granted and intended that we live.

Prosperity. Many relegate the meaning of prosperity to just money, but prosperity means much more. Prosperity means to "advance, to make progress, to go well." A person can have money and not understand money, so they spend their life pursuing money, rather than pursuing and serving God. When we focus on ministry and not money, *"God shall*

---

[94] https://www.gotquestions.org/pursue-righteousness.html. Accessed January 14, 2020.

supply all your need according to his riches in glory by Christ Jesus" (Philippians 4:19, KJV). Another translation of the word prosperity, according to *Strong's Complete Concordance of the Bible,* is *shalom,* which is "completeness, soundness, and welfare" with God and with people.

Honor. The Bible describes honor as "esteem, value, or great respect." To honor someone is to "value or to bestow value upon" them. The Bible speaks of honoring many types of people.

o   Give elders and leaders of the church double honor (1 Timothy 5:17).
o   Follow the directives of those who rule over you in employer/employee relationships (1 Timothy 3:17; 1 Timothy 6:1; Ephesians 6:5-9).
o   Respect your spouse and wife submit to husband (Hebrews 13:4; Ephesians 5:23-33).

Honor is sometimes synonymous with love. Paul commands us to *"be devoted to one another in brotherly love. Honor one another above yourselves"* (Romans 12:10). Honoring others, however, goes against our natural instinct to honor and value ourselves.

It is only by being cloaked in humility by the power of the Holy Spirit that we can esteem and honor our fellow man more than ourselves (Romans 12:3; Philippians 2:3). Proverbs 21:21 tells us that the result of pursuing God's righteousness is a life that bears fruit of life, prosperity, and honor. John's Gospel reminds us that we can bear fruit if we remain in Him:

> *"Remain in me, and I will remain in you. A branch can't produce fruit by itself, but must remain in the*

vine. Likewise, you can't produce fruit unless you remain in me. I am the vine; you are the branches. If you remain in me and I in you, then you will produce much fruit. Without me, you can't do anything" (John 15:4-5, CEB).

There is nothing that we can do in life or ministry without the presence and power of the Lord abiding within us! To remain is to stay in the same place, to continue to exist, or to stay behind after others have gone.

The New Living Translation of John 6:66-68 gives the account where Jesus' disciples remained when others left:

"At this point many of his disciples turned away and deserted him. Then Jesus turned to the Twelve and asked, "Are you also going to leave?" Simon Peter replied, "Lord, to whom would we go? You have the words that give eternal life."

Some will stay or remain with the Lord, while others will desert their relationship with Him. If we remain in the Lord, there is great spiritual treasure in pursuing God's righteousness. When we pursue righteousness in God, we find the truest treasures.

"My purpose is that they may be encouraged in heart and united in love, so that they may have the full riches of complete understanding, in order that they may know the mystery of God, namely, Christ, in whom are hidden all the treasures of wisdom and knowledge." (Colossians 2:2-3, NIV)

In conclusion, the truest treasures pertain to spiritual matters. The wisdom and knowledge of God are the greatest treasures that we can acquire as we learn to overcome negative thoughts by thinking like God thinks.

Think Like God Thinks: You Could Leave Life Right Now

According to James 4:14-15, "*You do not know what tomorrow will bring. What is your life? You are a mist that appears for a little while and then vanishes. Instead you should say, If the Lord wants us to, we will live — and do this or that.*" A vapor is a fine mist like fog. It quickly burns away when the sun comes up. It has no substance and leaves nothing behind. Comparing our lives to a vapor illustrates how fleeting our days on this earth are.

It is important to recognize the brevity of life so that we don't squander the time we've been given. During our brief stay on earth, we should live with eternity always before us. Jesus Himself felt the urgency of being about His Father's work while the opportunity remained. He said, "*As long as it is day, we must do the works of Him who sent me. Night is coming, when no one can work*" (John 9:4). The great commission of Matthew 28:19-20 should be at the forefront of the work for God's people.

> "*Therefore, go and make disciples of all nations, baptizing them in the name of the Father and of the Son and of the Holy Spirit, and teaching them to obey everything I have commanded you. And surely, I am with you always, to the very end of the age*" (ESV).

The passage essentially outlines what Jesus expected of the apostles then and what He expects of us now. The great commission instructs us to make disciples while we are going through the journey of life. God wants us to live life to its fullest.

Take that class! Enjoy vacation with your family, go to the theatre, buy that new house that you've been saving for! But always be cognizant that life is short, so we want to gather as many as possible into the Kingdom of God and make them disciples just like Jesus did. However, we cannot do what Jesus did until we learn to *think like God thinks!*

> *We cannot do what Jesus did until we learn to think like God thinks!*

Overcoming Negative Thoughts– Think Like God Thinks

To disciple someone, you must influence them by teaching and training them to live their best life, which is life in Jesus Christ! To make disciples of men, it is imperative that we overcome negative thinking by thinking like God thinks.

The Passion Translation of Romans 12:1-2 reads:

> *"Beloved friends, what should be our proper response to God's marvelous mercies? I encourage you to surrender yourselves to God to be his sacred, living sacrifices. And live in holiness, experiencing all that*

delights his heart. For this becomes your genuine expression of worship. Stop imitating the ideals and opinions of the culture around you, But be inwardly transformed by the Holy Spirit through a total reformation of how you think. This will empower you to discern God's will as you live a beautiful life, satisfying and perfect in his eyes."

We cannot think like the world; we must renew our minds. Thoughts are important! Scientist Lynn McTaggart notes that *"a thought is not only a thing; a thought is a thing that influences other things."*[95] We defined influence earlier in this book as the capacity to become *"a compelling, irresistible force that affects the actions, behavior, and conduct of others."* The influence of our thoughts is compelling and irresistible and where your mind goes your life will follow. What we think about what God thinks determines our future.

We must reform our minds so that we think like God thinks because It's All About Him! We must reform our minds so that we overcome negative thoughts and think like God thinks! My prayer is that as servants of the Lord Jesus Christ, you and I will serve the principles and precepts of this book to family members, co-workers, neighbors, friends and yes, even our enemies. I pray that as we practice the concepts that God has set forth in this book, that we begin to consistently and constantly learn how to overcome negative thoughts and think like God thinks.

As you think like God thinks, I encourage you to make every day your best day ever and live your life to the fullest

---

[95] Lynn McTaggart, The Intention Experiment: Using Your thoughts To Change Your life and The World (New York: Atria, 2008), Kindle loc.160-61.

for God's glory, other people's gain where it all works together for the good (Romans 8:28).

> *Make every day your best day ever as you learn to "Think Like God Thinks!" Isaiah 55:8-9*

Principles and Precepts For Transforming Our Thinking

"And do not be conformed to this world [any longer with its superficial values and customs], but be transformed and progressively changed [as you mature spiritually] by the renewing of your mind [focusing on godly values and ethical attitudes], so that you may prove [for yourselves] what the will of God is, that which is good and acceptable and perfect [in His plan and purpose for you]" (Romans 12:2, AMP).

Principle-a universal law that is true in any context, situation, or environment.

Precept-life lessons indicating the way one should act or behave.

Practice-the act of rehearsing a behavior over and over, for the purpose of improving or mastering it.

Chapter 9 Reflection Practices

1. When we visualize achievements such as losing weight by exercising, getting the promotion, obtaining that pay raise, saving for that house, being more grateful and thankful, we are thinking like God thinks. Natural science and research validate that when we see it and conceive it by faith, we reprogram our brains.[96]
    This is the place where we change the filters of how and what we think.

    o Take a few moments each day to visualize achieving your goals.
    o If you need assistance forgetting the past, ask God for a mindset of reset.
    o Apply reflective thinking and the other principles and precepts in this chapter to redirect negative thoughts.

2. Read over the sections discussing how we should honor others and be slow to speak and quick to hear. Study the related scriptures (James 1:19; 1 Timothy 5:17; 1 Timothy 3:17; Ephesians 6:5-9; Hebrews 13:4; Ephesians 5:23-33). Make a conscious effort to practice these principles this week.

---

[96] https://www.ncbi.nlm.nih.gov/pmc/articles/PMC2802367/. Accessed January 13, 2020.

EPILOGUE

Bishop Roderick Mitchell
New Life Church, Cleveland, Mississippi

(Genesis 2:10-14) *"And a river went out of Eden to water the garden; and from thence it was parted and became into four heads. The name of the first is Pison: that is it which compasseth the whole land of Havilah, where there is gold; And the gold of that land is good: there is bdellium and the onyx stone. And the name of the second river is Gihon: the same is it that compasseth the whole land of Ethiopia. And the name of the third river is Hiddekel: that is it which goeth toward the east of Assyria. And the fourth river is Euphrates."*

(Psalms 1:1-3 Living Bible) *"Oh, the joys of those who do not follow evil men's advice, who do not hang around with sinners, scoffing at the things of God. But they delight in doing everything God wants them to, and day and night are always meditating on his laws and* **"THINKING"** *about ways to follow him more closely.*

They are like trees planted by the **rivers of waters** *bearing luscious fruit each season without fail. Their leaves shall never wither, and all they do shall prosper."* The preceding passages of Scripture speak to the nature of this book as given by the Holy Spirit. In the Genesis account, it speaks of how the river went out of Eden but at some point, parted. The parting of the river became *"four*

161

heads," that touched different areas or parts of the earth. Each head flowed from the original river that went out of Eden. Each area of the earth was watered by the original river in Eden, even though it came in a part. *Overcoming Negative Thoughts-Think Like God Thinks* is a part of the knowledge of God (*Eden*), given to us by the Holy Spirit (*The River*) through Dr. Gregory L. Cruell (*parted from The River-a head*). As the people of God planted by *"the rivers of waters"* (Psalm 1:3), reflecting upon this information imparted by the Holy Spirit, we will find ourselves *"thinking"* about ways that strengthens our ability to *"follow Him more closely"* (Psalm 1:2).

Despite the negative experiences and negative thoughts that challenge us daily, the Bible instructs us that in *"all our getting we are to get understanding"* (Proverbs 4:7). Therefore, throughout this book, we have been given understanding that aligns ourselves with the Living Word of God, Christ Jesus, our Lord, which as we *"follow Him more closely,"* causes us to *"Think Like God Thinks."* Consider this which was spoken by our Lord in John 16:33, the Living Bible. *"I have told you all this so that you will have peace of heart and mind. Here on earth you will have many trials and sorrows; but cheer up, for I have overcome the world."*

Jesus shares with us that living in this earth includes trials and sorrows, that are always accompanied by negative thinking. The trials and sorrows which Jesus spoke of concerning the presence of negativity in the world, is also spoken of in the Genesis account of the creation.

Consider this as recorded in Genesis 1:4-5. *"And God saw the light, that it was good: and God divided the light from the darkness. And God called the light Day, and the darkness he called Night. And the evening and the morning were the first day."*(Genesis 1:16-18) *"And God made two great lights; the greater light to rule the day, and the lesser light to rule the night: he made the stars also. And God set them in the firmament of the heaven to give light upon the earth, and to rule over the day and over the night, and to divide the light from the darkness: and God saw that it was good."*

From the perspective of this epilogue, light represents positive or godly thinking. Darkness represents negative or ungodly thinking. In the dividing of light from darkness, they were separated one from the other, but both were still present. Please note, God provided two great lights, one greater than the other, but both had authority to rule over what they were in the midst of.

Overcoming Negative Thoughts–Thinking Like God Thinks, helps us to understand that although darkness or negative thinking may be present, but provision has been made to overcome it, by ruling over it, with the light (God's Word) that has been given unto us as God's people!

Four Heads (*Thoughts*) of The River (Genesis 2:10-14)

<u>Head–(*Thought*)#1</u>

Negative thinking is an experience of life that we will all encounter. Thinking like God thinks encourages us to not just **go through it**, but to **grow through it!** Negative thinking says, give up, let the pressure and pain of your predicament overwhelm you! Thinking like a God thinks says, don't let it be **wasted pain**; let it be **working pain**. The pressures and pains are not there to stop you, they're there to prepare you, to increase you, to develop, shape and mold you.

The Scripture teaches us how God is in control, not just of our lives, but He's in control of our enemies. Psalms 27:1-2, *"The Lord is my light and my salvation; whom shall I fear? the Lord* is the strength of my life; of whom shall I be afraid? When the wicked, even mine enemies and my foes, came upon me to eat up my flesh, they stumbled and fell."

The enemy may turn up the heat, but the good news is, **God has his hand on the thermostat!** God controls how much heat, how much pain, and how much adversity that we can handle. If it was going to harm us rather than help us, God would have turned back the intensity. 1 Corinthians 10:13 declares that, *"there hath no temptation taken you but such as is common to man: but God is faithful, who will not suffer you to be tempted above that ye are able; but will with the temptation also make a way to escape, that ye may be able to bear it."* Living through negative experiences, that produce negative thoughts, provides growth because we know that **God still has hand on the thermostat and I'm growing on!**

Head–(*Thought*)#2

The making of the "PEARL" gives us additional insight as to how thinking like God thinks enables us to overcome negative thoughts. The beauty of a single pearl, or a string of the precious stones, is unmistakable.

Few jewels capture the eye quite like a perfect pearl. In the beginning, the pearl is only a grain of sand. That tiny little grain of sand, then slips inside the tight seal of an oyster's shell, and immediately causes discomfort (*a form of negative experiences producing negative thinking*) to the oyster. With no way to expel the grain of sand, with no way to ease the pain, the oyster coats the sand with a layer of the inner lining of its shell to make the sand smooth. This still does not ease the oyster's suffering. Again, and again the oyster coats the sand, but all the attempts to get rid of the discomfort and irritation have little effect. As far as an oyster is concerned, what we call a "pearl" is nothing more than great suffering! But one day the oyster is fished from the water and opened.

The gem inside has amazing beauty and holds great value – all because the oyster, continued to coat the sand, that was the irritant, with the inner lining of the shell. As it is for the oyster, so is it for you and me. The oyster's persistent irritant (*negative experiences producing negative thinking*) through perseverance turned into something valuable and beautiful! The Voice Translation of Romans 8:28 reminds us that, *"we are confident that God is able to orchestrate everything to work toward something good and beautiful when we love Him and accept His invitation to live according to His plan."* It's hard to imagine that something irritating and frustrating can become something valuable and beautiful. But as we learn to think like God thinks, He makes the things that frustrate us and irritate us to work together for the good according to His plan.

Head–(*Thought*)#3

Negative thinking has the potential to say, *"God must not be with you, look at the pain that you FEEL."*

If the presence of God is with us, we would not **FEEL** depressed, disillusioned, discouraged, and disheartened. Thinking like God thinks declares that you don't have to *feel* Christ to know that He is with you. The Bible records in the New International Version of Genesis 28:16, *"Jacob awoke out of his sleep, and he said, "Surely the LORD is in this place, and I did not know it."* Jesus says in Matthew 28:20, *"I am with you always, even to the end of the age."* If we are His follower, Christ's straightforward promise is that He will be with us and will see us through every aspect of life until the very end of the world.

His ways are higher than ours. He knows the length of our days and has our next steps prepared. When we think like God thinks, the Holy Spirit reminds us that He has a plan for our lives. In that plan that He has for our lives we must determine that we will not be hindered by heartaches, struggles, sicknesses, death of a loved one, family problems, financial problems or any other problem that knocks on our door!

God's love never stops, and the troubles of this world do not define us! Yet, the trouble that we endure are necessary tools to develop our character and conduct for curtailing the efforts of the enemy who tries to perpetually stop faith in God from working powerfully in our lives! James 1:2-4, in the Living Bible proclaims," *Dear brothers, is your life full of difficulties and temptations? Then be happy, for when the way is rough, your patience has a chance to grow. So let it grow, and **don't try to squirm out of your problems. For when your patience is finally in full bloom, then you will be ready for anything, strong in character, full and complete.***"

Therefore, thinking like God thinks, empower us, *"to endure hardness, as a good soldier of Jesus Christ"* (2 Timothy 2:3). It was A.W. Tozer that once wrote, *"It is doubtful whether God can bless a man greatly until he has wounded him deeply."* Tozer understood that the trials allowed by God are meant to bless and equip the soldier of Christ for perpetual victory.

Head–(*Thought*)#4

As we mature in our walk with the Lord and we do not allow negative thinking to overcome us, continuing to learn to think as God thinks, our spirit, soul and body are always open to the **process of growth**. (1 Peter 2:2-3) *"You've had a taste of God. Now, like infants at the breast, drink deep of God's pure kindness. Then you'll **grow up mature** and whole in God."* (2 Peter 3:18) *"**But grow in spiritual strength** and become better acquainted with our Lord and Savior Jesus Christ. To him be all glory and splendid honor, both now and forevermore."*

(Ephesians 4:15) *"But speaking the truth in love, **may grow up** into him in all things, which is the head, even Christ."* (2 Timothy 2:7) *"Consider what I say, and the Lord give thee understanding in all things."* Consider the growth and development of the Lotus Flower. The lotus flower represents an awakening, spiritual growth, and enlightenment. The lotus is the most beautiful flower, whose petals open one by one. But it will only **grow in the mud!**

In order to grow and gain wisdom, we must first have the mud — the obstacles of life and its suffering. The lotus flower grows in muddy water and rises above the surface to bloom with remarkable beauty! The lotus flower can be found all over the world. It is unlike many other flowers. When the lotus first begins to sprout, it is under water, making its home in lakes and ponds in areas where the water remains still on the surface. But underneath the surface, the lotus is surrounded by mud and muck and by fish, by insects, and simply dirty, rough conditions. Despite these conditions, the lotus flower maintains strength, and pushes aside each of these dirty obstacles as it makes its way to clearer surfaces. At this time, the lotus is still just a stem with only a few leaves, and a small flower pod. But in time, the stem continues to grow, and the pod slowly surfaces above the water, into the clean air, finally freeing itself from the harsh life conditions below.

It is then that the lotus slowly opens each of its beautiful petals to the sun, basking in a triumphant entrance into the world, the lotus flower is now ready to take on the world! Despite being born into dark, muddy, murky conditions, where hope for such a beautiful life seems doubtful, the lotus grows, and rises above adversity. Ironically, the same dirty water that the lotus had to push through, now washes it clean as it surfaces. As the lotus opens each petal to the air, not a stain or spot of mud remains externally. The inner lotus too, has never seen a drop of mud or dirty water. It is pure, and bright, and beautiful. The lotus flower represents an *awakening, spiritual growth, and enlightenment!* Just as the lotus flower emerges from the water clean, the lotus also represents purity of body, speech, and mind. The lotus could be thought of as an awakened mind, which grows naturally toward the warmth and light of truth, love and compassion.

The lotus may appear fragile on the surface, but it is flexible and strong, securely anchored under the surface of the water. We are all like the lotus flower. Many have lived in muddy, murky water, and never make it to the surface to blossom because of negative thinking. No matter what stage of life we may be in, the story of the lotus is our story. The conditions that produce a beautiful life, an abundant life, are not always ideal, but that never stops the lotus from rising through adversity, opening its petals, and blossoming in the sun! You may be facing a murky, muddy water situation presently, and it seems like that you are never going to blossom.

Know that you are more valuable to God than the lotus flower! And if God allows the lotus flower to blossom in the mud, He won't do any less for you. You may have complained, you may have cried, due to negative experiences that have produced negative thoughts, but remember that the *lotus will only grow and bloom in the mud!*

David declares in Psalm 40:1-3 in the Message Bible, *"I waited and waited and waited for GOD. At last he looked; finally, He listened. He lifted me out of the ditch,* **pulled me from deep mud.** *He stood me up on a solid rock to make sure I wouldn't slip. He taught me how to sing the latest God-song, a praise-song to our God. More and more people are seeing this: they enter the mystery, abandoning themselves to GOD."*

Overcoming Negative Thoughts–Thinking Like God Thinks enables us to push through the mud, to blossom and bloom, doing better day by day. The Passion Translation of 1 Peter 1:13 teaches us to, *"prepare your **hearts and minds** for action! Stay alert and fix your hope firmly on the marvelous grace that is coming to you. For when Jesus Christ is unveiled, a **greater measure of grace will be released to you**."* There are two lights, darkness (*negative thinking*) and the greater light (*Thinking Like God Thinks*), the light of God's Word that overcomes the darkness.

Preparing our *hearts* and *minds* for action as Peter exhorts in the preceding passage is our part of the spiritual warfare for overcoming negative thoughts. It is a never ending battle, fought daily. The nature of this book, *Overcoming Negative Thoughts–Thinking Like God Thinks,* helps us to understand that darkness or negative thinking will always be present, but provision has been made to overcome negative thoughts, ruling over them, with the light of God's Word that has been given unto us. And as *"Christ is unveiled, a greater measure of grace will be released to us"* (1 Peter 1:13) to the glory of God! It's All About Him, Jesus, That's What It's All About!

Notes: _____

Notes: _____

Notes: _____

Download your free copy of the *T.H.I.N.K. TOOL*. This 5-step process is designed to move us all closer of the ideal to *"THINK LIKE GOD THINKS.* (Isaiah 55:8-9)

Get your free copy at: www.gregorycruell.com/thinktool

Additional Publications By Dr. Cruell

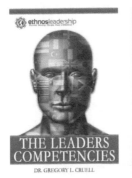

Visit us at www.gregorycruell.com or contact us via email at info@gregorycruell.com